Praise for
CALM WITHIN THE STORM

"In the approachable and often poetic style that defines her work, Dr. Robyne Hanley-Dafoe illustrates that resiliency isn't some ideal state achieved through suffering and scars; it's a built-in feature of being a human. As unflinching as it is insightful, this book will permanently alter how you see yourself and your ability to endure."
DR. GREG WELLS, physiologist and researcher at SickKids, bestselling author, and keynote speaker

"Dr. Robyne Hanley-Dafoe hits the nail square on the head. More than twenty years of expedition experience has taught me that resiliency is not an exclusive realm, reserved only for the uber-tough and fearless. Rather, this life-changing trait is available to every single one of us—in spades. In this systematic yet deeply felt book, Dr. Hanley-Dafoe lays out a simple framework that will revolutionize how you engage with all of life's adversities."
BRUCE KIRKBY, Canadian adventurer, author, and photographer

"Dr. Robyne Hanley-Dafoe has created an insightful, smart, and thought-provoking (yet practical!) manual for redefining resiliency in everyday life. This is a book that you can revisit when you're overwhelmed, in a growth period of your life, or when helping young people navigate their own path."
SILKEN LAUMANN, Olympian and mental health advocate

"This written record of resiliency is replete with a mountain of motivation and acres of encouragement. Dr. Robyne Hanley-Dafoe poignantly portrays her personal adolescent struggles with mental health and takes us by the hand through an intentional, sustainable pathway to mental wealth. Practical, educational, inspiring … phenomenal!"

MICHAEL "PINBALL" CLEMONS, Canadian Football and Canadian Sports Hall of Famer

"Amazing and inspiring! *Calm Within the Storm* helps us to view and navigate the challenges of life with more understanding and positive perspective while simultaneously encouraging us to see ourselves as innately capable of overcoming and working through adversity, setbacks, and success to live resiliency daily. This is not an instructional self-help book—it is a book of empowerment and an invitation to a deeper connection with yourself. Dr. Robyne Hanley-Dafoe's balance of vulnerability with personal stories, assurance through research and studies, and a passionate but light-hearted desire to uplift others wrap this book in good vibes and positive feels. Sit back, read, learn about your resilient self, and *bounce back*!"

CAVELL JOHNSON, NBL All-Star, coach and GM of the KW Titans, and former NCAA Basketball Division I player

"Using story and science, Dr. Robyne Hanley-Dafoe's book provides insight to help you find whatever you are searching for. Just like her dynamic speaking style, her writing pops off the page and speaks to your heart and your head. *Calm Within the Storm* equips you with the skills needed to tackle challenges in these difficult times."

BRIAN CALLAHAN, president and COO of ISN

"Dr. Robyne Hanley-Dafoe has spent over twenty years becoming a renowned expert in resiliency. Read this book, and you'll become one in a significantly shorter time. I devoured every page and loved every word. You will too."

RON TITE, founder and CEO of Church+State, host and executive producer of *The Coup*, and author of *Think. Do. Say.*

"Dr. Robyne Hanley-Dafoe writes with a profound mastery not only of the scientific research, but also of narrative voice. You feel her gentle, encouraging, and utterly human self guiding you as you read. She moves from gripping story, to case study, to science-based research, to tangible action items and take-aways so seamlessly that it allows you to have both your heart and mind opened while your soul breathes with a knowing that there is—and will always be—a way forward for you. This book is a lighthouse for each of us on our journey to resiliency and will surely be held up as a definitive work on the subject alongside the likes of Brené Brown, Glennon Doyle, and Viktor Frankl."

PETER KATZ, award-winning singer and songwriter

"Dr. Robyne Hanley-Dafoe is a powerful force when it comes to wanting to get your life back on track! A must-read and an inspiring outlook on how to move forward in life. Her story is an inspiration."

ELIZABETH MANLEY, Olympic champion, mental health advocate, and life coach

"*Calm Within the Storm* is your guide to building your resiliency. Dr. Robyne Hanley-Dafoe has written a practical and accessible book about her journey that is compelling right from the opening pages. Grounded in research and honed by years of practice in the field, Dr. Hanley-Dafoe's new model presents a clear and easy path to building resiliency. This book is a game changer."

DR. IVAN JOSEPH, award-winning performance and self-confidence coach and VP of student affairs at Wilfrid Laurier University

"Life finds curious ways to remind us that uncertainty is our only certainty. *Calm Within the Storm* offers an invitation to meet ourselves where we are. Dr. Robyne Hanley-Dafoe reframes resiliency as a reconnection with our true self. She encourages us to believe that we all hold the capacity to be worthy and enough."

RICK HANSEN, track and field athlete and founder of the Rick Hansen Foundation

CALM
WITHIN
— THE —
STORM

CALM
WITHIN
—— THE ——
STORM

A Pathway to
Everyday Resiliency

DR. ROBYNE HANLEY-DAFOE

●● **PAGE TWO** BOOKS

Some names and identifying details have been
changed to protect the privacy of individuals.

This book is not intended as a substitute for the medical
advice of physicians or mental health professionals.
The reader should consult a physician or mental health
professional in matters relating to their physical or mental
health and particularly with respect to any symptoms
that may require diagnosis or medical attention.

Cataloguing in publication information
is available from Library and Archives Canada.
ISBN 978-1-989603-87-1 (hardcover)
ISBN 978-1-989603-88-8 (ebook)

Page Two
www.pagetwo.com

Edited by Amanda Lewis
Copyedited by Steph VanderMeulen
Proofread by Alison Strobel
Jacket and interior design by Jennifer Lum
Printed and bound in Canada by Friesens
Distributed in Canada by Raincoast Books
Distributed in the US and internationally by
Publishers Group West, a division of Ingram

21 22 23 24 25   5 4 3 2 1

robynehd.ca

This book is dedicated to my mom.

She believed in me, so one day I could believe in myself.

And to Hunter, Ava Lesley, and Jaxson.

Thank you for loving me back.

I respectfully acknowledge that this work was written upon the treaty and traditional territory of the Michi Saagiig Anishinaabeg. I am a settler in this space. I offer my gratitude and give thanks to the people who have walked before me.

CALM

WITHIN

— THE —

STORM

INTRODUCTION

Truly Okay 1

PART I: THE COMEBACK

1 The Sentence 13

2 Resiliency Redefined 29

PART II: THE THREE OBSTACLES

3 Stress 49

4 Fear 67

5 Stigma 87

PART III: THE FIVE PILLARS
THE BASELINE FOR RESILIENCY

6 Belonging 105

7 Perspective 125

8 Acceptance 143

9 Hope 159

10 Humour 181

PART IV: THE PATHS

11 The Resiliency Trajectory Model 207

12 The Four Phases 219

13 Worth 243

CONCLUSION

Lighthouses 257

Acknowledgements 269

Notes 275

Index 285

"The sun will never reveal as much about yourself as the storm does."

JMSTORM

"

Just because you carry it well,
doesn't mean it is not heavy.

"

TRULY OKAY

"YOU ARE GOING to be okay." That is the most common statement made by first responders when they come upon someone in distress or at the scene of an accident. Hearing those words can de-escalate someone from panic and fear, and even subdue pain. Why is it that being okay in most other circumstances is not good enough? Yet in life or death moments, the words, "You're okay" or "they are going to be okay" are a lifeline?

"Okay" is absolutely everything. It is all that truly matters. Okay and being okay are at the heart of true resiliency.

This book is an invitation to reframe how we think about resiliency. Often associated with concepts like persistence, mental toughness, or grit, resiliency is portrayed as a battle cry to summon Herculean strength. This forceful understanding and practice of resiliency is not attainable or sustainable for many of us. Life is hard, and it continues to be hard, but bearing down and pushing through the pain is not the only way to navigate the bumps, bruises, setbacks, and heartache. White-knuckling pain is not the only option.

Resiliency to me means doing the next right thing. It is taking that precarious step in the direction you want to go, despite what the world says about you or how hard it might be.

Unlike the current resiliency landscape that yells at us that we are not doing it right, or we just have to get over it, this book introduces a new theory of resiliency—what I call everyday resiliency. My theory of resiliency is based on years of experience working with people all around the globe as an educator, coach, and counsellor. I never intended to create a new theory. My intention was to support people through their life's journey. To welcome people where they were and help them map a course for where they could go. To help people see who they could become, and live a life that reflected their truest self. I think Ram Dass said it best when he wrote, "When all is said and done, we're all just walking each other home."[1]

The ultimate goal of everyday resiliency is to foster a deep and personal sense of being okay, no matter what. I want you to discover that what you already have in your head and heart makes you capable of meeting any obstacle and rising to any challenge. With this steadfast self-awareness, you will live with the conviction that you are okay, and you will be okay. Rather than being at the top of your game or perfect all the time, you'll realize that being okay is truly enough.

I have spent the last two decades instructing and learning alongside people from all walks of life. I have worked with them from early infanthood to elderhood as they navigated trials, tribulations, challenges, and setbacks.

Personally, I have spent time in the shadows of society as well. I have had my own mental health challenges, learning blocks, disordered eating behaviours, pain, abuse, loss, grief, and worst of all, the stigma that comes with those labels. As a psychology and education instructor, I have spent most of my career studying, teaching, and applying what we know about psychology as a means of helping people out of the shadows of pain through the practices of resiliency while personally trying to find my own way out, too. During this parallel journey, what I came upon was truly unique. I saw patterns, themes, and tendencies that forged a deeper understanding of what resiliency truly is. I experienced first-hand that resiliency theories, in general, needed a reckoning. So, here it is.

Resiliency is not reserved only for the mentally tough, the strong, or the fearless. Each person has the capacity for resiliency. It is not something you have or do not have. It is not something you are born with. When a person lives an examined life, they come upon this knowledge. When they know where to look, a person can see just how truly equipped they are to deal with all of life's pains. Resiliency is there, inside us, and needs to be recognized. The most common reflection I hear from people who have survived life's cruellest and hardest moments is, "I never knew I could survive this." But they did. And you will, too.

I think of my approach as everyday resiliency because the small decisions we make each day set up our ability to do the extraordinary: the big hurts, losses, setbacks, and traumas. I believe that anyone can be extraordinary when they already experience everyday resiliency in their interactions with the world. Everyday resiliency becomes a tool that aligns with our primal drive to feel safe and secure.

Our physical, emotional, and mental health are being taxed and tested every single day. There is an extraordinary need to build, foster, and practice resiliency so we can navigate the most basic parts of our lives. Yet, we live in a social ecosystem that has adopted the belief that, at any given moment, doing any given thing, we are supposed to be better, faster, smarter, richer, stronger—everything "-er." There is an underlying pressure to be doing it better, or that *we* should be better. The feeling persists that there is a right way to do life, and if it is hard, then it is because we are doing it wrong. We are broken.

Morality is somehow interwoven with performance, accomplishments, and success—when we fail, we are "bad." Comparison and judgement run rampant. We're all compelled to live our best lives, but we receive constant messaging that we are not.

Or perhaps you are carrying around an old story that has you stuck. I have worked with leaders of the largest organizations in the world, leaders who have shared with me stories of shame, of not being enough, of feeling like an imposter, and of not knowing how they ended up sitting at these tables or how they are responsible for such massive decisions. I have worked with high-performance athletes who from the outside seem to have perfected resiliency, dedication, and toughness, and who have also reached the top echelon of their sports, but when alone share they feel undeserving, unsatisfied, or even not good enough. It seems like we are plagued with feelings of not being good enough or okay, and we cannot seem to strike that balance of truly being okay in our lives.

For some of us, this elusive state of not being okay may come from the outside world, through constant chaos, change, and pressure. And for some of us, the chaos comes from within: me versus myself. The personal war, in my opinion, is the most dangerous to our capacity for resiliency. It is easier to fight an enemy you can see, like a difficult boss, a challenging experience, or a health crisis. The hardest fight is within your own mind, body, and soul. When parts of you and how you see the world are your own worst enemy, part of you must fall for the other part to rise.

FROM BASELINE TO RISING

Before we jump into the research and practices for engaging in these internal and external battles for navigating resiliency, I want to share a bit more about me, the person behind this work. Yes, I am a scholar in psychology and education who has worked in the academy, or higher education, but not in the traditional sense. I am not sitting in the ivory tower pontificating about what we know about resiliency from the world of academia. I am an outsider because I learned this topic from the ground up as I rose from the ashes of my former self.

My learning happened outside of textbooks. Today I still feel as though I have more in common with the angsty teenager and those who also walked through the shadows than I do with professors. My career brought me to the academy, but I am only stopping by. I have worked in a university for nearly fourteen years, but my non-linear route to getting here will always keep me as an outsider. And I am totally okay with that. My goal in school was never to become a professor and stay there—my deepest desire was to get there, break down the walls for others to follow, and then go back to the trenches and do the real "heart" work. I never just want to write or teach about resiliency; I want to help carry the load by making research and lessons accessible to those who need them most.

I am not just a researcher and educator. I am a person who has walked many paths. I have stumbled. I define my success by how many times I kept going despite the stumbles, pain, and hurt.

My days are filled with opportunities, privileges, and a deep sense of purpose and meaning. I never in my wildest dreams imagined that this life would be available to me. I feel loved; I can love; I am enough. My head, heart, and values are finally aligned. I am surrounded by family: a loving and supportive husband, Jeff; three children, Hunter, Ava Lesley, and Jaxson, with whom I am completely and totally in love; two playful puppies, Luna and Apollo; and even three wee rescue cats. We all share this bright and joy-filled life together. Our own little clan. Dear friendships and meaningful opportunities to be of service to others fill my days. I never dared to imagine what forty-one-year-old Robyne's life would look like because for most of my adolescence I was told I would not see eighteen years old.

Often when I work with people, they say things like, "It's easy for you to research resiliency because you are healthy, strong, and have everything together." From the outside, people make judgements about me fairly quickly. But that's before they realize they are seeing a work in progress that has spanned most of my adult life. So, my reply usually goes something like, "Just because I am carrying it well, doesn't mean it is not heavy."

People have tried to use my past against me. I tried to distance myself from my teenage years because they held so much embarrassment, shame, guilt, and hurt. As a former grade eleven high school dropout, I put ten years of university education, including a doctoral degree, between who I was then and who I am now. Interestingly, running away from who I was motivated me to achieve some ambitious goals, but when I met those goals, I did not feel fulfilled. I found fulfillment only when I realized I had been enough all along.

Once I realized that I did not need to prove anything to anyone, especially not to the people who told me I was not enough or that I was broken, my life started to change. Once I started to see and believe in my own worth, those who did not see and believe the same became irrelevant. Those voices and the power I let others hold over me evaporated. I took back the pen from stigma and past-shaming and started writing my own story.

Everyone possesses varying degrees of capacity for resiliency. I don't believe that resiliency is only a mindset; instead, it is our deep self-efficacy or confidence in our abilities. Resiliency is not simply bouncing back; it is also the steadfast belief that we can and will navigate the hard parts of our lives, no matter what. This book gives you a map to do just that.

THE EVERYDAY RESILIENCY ROAD MAP

Part I presents some of my personal story and struggle with resiliency. It is my origin story, so to speak. It answers why I study resiliency and how I got into this line of work. It is important for me to share with you that I am not your traditional expert. I am a person who has walked, stumbled, got back up, and tried to make the next right decision. I still have work to do too. I have made mistakes. I have regrets. And I also have learning, knowledge, understanding, and insight. I might even be tiptoeing close to wisdom in a few wee areas. One of the most amazing insights I can share with you is that both extremes of these experiences can coexist. My setbacks do not preclude my validity as a scholar, just as your mistakes do not define you. No one should be judged by their mistakes, weaknesses, or struggles.

It is fascinating how people tend to hold us in the chapter of our lives that they happened to walk in on, or that included them. The reality is that we are all a constellation of experiences—some good, some not so good—that make up who we are. So, I made the decision to get raw and real in some of my early chapters. These stories are crucial to how I understand resiliency and to my work as a practitioner. Alongside my story, I will also present a lay of the land about resiliency in broad strokes. I will touch on how resiliency studies started, and how we consider and use resiliency today.

Part II examines the common barriers to a resilient approach to living. I start with the problems that create the barriers: Why does life feel so hard? Why does life hurt? Why do so many of us seem to live in a constant state of strife and chaos? We seek peace, yet are drawn into drama. I will present the three most common variables that tend to get in the way of everyday resiliency, for people all around the world. No one is immune to difficulty and pain, but there is a means to address these underlying tendencies that derail us and keep us stuck.

In Part III, I get to the heart of resiliency. What do resilient people do differently? Where do they draw their strength and focus? Research shows that there are five interconnected pillars that are universal across cultures and backgrounds: belonging, perspective, acceptance, hope, and humour. These pillars form a person's capacity for resilient behaviours. I will introduce my model of resiliency through these five interconnected pillars, which establish our baseline for coping with life's challenges.

Part IV introduces you to my Resiliency Trajectory Model by showing you resiliency in action. It invites you to follow a series of paths that others have walked before you, which can serve as a guide as you strive for alignment within your whole self. I conclude this part of the book with a chapter devoted to self-esteem and self-worth. Although not a direct external barrier like the three discussed in Part II, self-esteem left unexamined can become an internal barrier that will impact your capacity to be resilient.

Embedded within each chapter are stories, research, and practical strategies woven together to produce wise practices. These wise practices are those teachable moments, those learn-by-trying experiences, that help you develop, expand, and strengthen your foundation of everyday resiliency.

SET YOUR INTENTION FOR THIS BOOK

Borrowed courage and real courage produce the same result: you keep going. So, here is my invitation. Please take a moment to set your intention as you read this book. What are you searching for? Are you looking for strategies to become more resilient? Are you hoping to support others in their journey of resiliency? Are you looking for peace, understanding, insight, or answers? Are you looking for courage? Are you searching for ideas about embracing change? Are you hoping to connect with and awaken that part of you that once felt whole? Or are you just as lost as I was, navigating uncharted territory? Regardless of why you are here, you are here. That matters. Just calling to mind what you are looking toward raises your awareness and helps you recognize your need when you read it.

Here is the deal: if you know what you are looking for, great—I hope you find it. If you do not know why you are here, that is perfectly okay too. I hope you will come upon something you need to hear. My goal as an educator is to share that piece of knowledge you need to hear, exactly when you need to hear it most. Our paths have now crossed. I welcome you as you are. Thank you for joining me.

PART I

— THE —

COMEBACK

"

I can do hard things.

"

CHAPTER 1

THE SENTENCE

WHAT SENTENCE WOULD sum up your life? Usually people ponder such questions in elderhood, when they look back on their life and reflect on how they might sum it up. Well, I was born into a sentence, and I am ever so grateful. It changed my world, and I believe it will change the world for others as well.

In 2019, I had the honour of teaming up with the non-profit group Unsinkable (weareunsinkable.com). The community was created by decorated Canadian Olympian Silken Laumann. Laumann created a space where people could share their stories on a public platform. Her mission was to connect and empower Canadians to achieve better mental, physical, and spiritual health. Whether celebrity, neighbour, youth, or health expert, Laumann believes that our stories all hold wisdom and power that needs to be shared. Unsinkable is breaking down stigma, one story at a time.

I was invited to write an article for the Unsinkable website that recounted my story of surviving a horrific car crash at sixteen years old. When I sat down to write about my experience, I realized that surviving the accident was significant, but what was also significant was overcoming the stigma and mental health challenges I had carried since I was a child. At some point in my childhood, I started occupying two lanes. In one lane I was on track, successful, healthy, and competent. And somehow, concurrently, I was also in another lane. I was troubled, lost, and hurting. My public self was doing all right by most standards. My private self was spiralling wildly out of control.

By adolescence, my invisible struggles became very visible. And with that visibility came the labels: "high school dropout," "broken," "addicted," "eating disordered," "cutter," "crazy," "troubled," "lost cause." These labels accompanied the internal labels I gave myself. I deduced I was unworthy of the abundant love, support, and faith of my parents. I was a *disappointment* and *undeserving.* I concluded I was an utter failure and hopeless. *Unlovable.* I carried such deep and soul-damaging stigma about the person I was. The stigma first came from the outside world. The world presented a set of norms that did not fit me. Then pressures and judgements came from people directly. I was judged, ridiculed, gaslighted, mistreated, and ostracized for struggling in many life areas. My parents loved me hard and helplessly.

People say that surviving the car accident was a miracle, and I agree. My life was spared that night. Over two decades later, I am awestruck by the realization that the night of my accident, my miracle was already in motion. But there is a dark side to my miracle story, and I carried that part for many years. This painful question haunted me in my sleep and when I was wide awake: *Did I deserve this miracle?* I knew the answer, but I would not ever dare let my head go there.

I did not.

I know when my car went off the road that night, but when had my life gone off-track? Why would I believe that I did not deserve to be rescued?

When I was in grade eight, a teacher in my elementary school told me, as I was filling out my forms for grade nine, that I really should not even try to go to the same high school as my peers. That teacher told me that I was so far behind in French, I would be a disgrace to my elementary school's French Immersion program if I went to the French high school. They also told me that they wished there was a level below "Basic" or "Trades" for someone like me to take in high school since I wasn't ever going to amount to anything in life, and all I would be doing is wasting everyone's time. School hated me, and I hated it right back. I believed every word of that teacher's assessment of me and the world's perspective of me. But how did I end up in grade eight with a teacher who would say this to me?

It would be so much easier if I could pinpoint one event that caused this derailment as a child, but there really wasn't one. Instead, it was the stories I told myself about me, which I believed were true. I sought evidence from the world, and I could always find evidence to support my negative narrative. I could also just as quickly discount the mountains of evidence that could correct my fractured view of myself. It seemed that I was destined to feel everything to my core. The negative feelings that I fought to keep in the shadows eventually started creeping into the daylight hours. I learned how to armour up, wear masks, and assimilate according to what situations asked of me. I became a social chameleon everywhere I went. But despite my best efforts to hide the hurting parts, I found myself in a steady emotional decline from grades six to eleven. Six years is a long time to white-knuckle parts of your life, but somehow I did just that.

I had devoted and loving parents who created a great life for me. I had a great childhood. And within that great childhood, I picked up this self-narrative that would eventually lead me off the path my parents had created for me. I know other families can relate to this. You did everything right, yet your child still went off-course. Perhaps one sibling soared and the other floundered even though they grew up in the same household. Many people who go off-track have specific elements within their story, called "social determinants of health," that can explain or could have predicted their way-wardness. The World Health Organization defines social determinants of health as known conditions in which people are born, grow, work, live, and age, and the wider set of forces and systems shaping the conditions of daily life.[1] These forces and systems have an impact on the health and wellness of people. Our environments matter—they shape us. Interesting examples of social determinants of health include a mother's education, which is known to predict a child's education level more than the father's; living below the poverty line, which contributes to poor health conditions; and reading to a toddler, which improves literacy and language acquisition.

In my case, all my social determinants of health and wellness were in check and exceeded the daily requirements, so to speak, but I still found a way to go off-course. My parents' love, support, and guidance could not, in the moment, protect me from myself. I remember my first experiences of feeling like an outsider as early as kindergarten. As early as six years old, I felt excluded; I felt "othered" somehow. I felt deep shame but didn't know what it was. I was embarrassed for my parents. They deserved a better daughter. My vivid imagination and constant mental narrative decided I was the problem. By grade one, I concluded that my family loved me because they had to, not because they wanted to. I felt unlovable at times. My otherness was reinforced by my body taking up too much space—my weight, freckles, red hair, learning challenges, and an inability to keep friends. My desperate attempts to fit in pushed people away. I loved my life, but I did not love me in it. What is amazing about a childhood is that you can have multiple perspectives happening concurrently. While feeling like an outsider and unlovable, I could also have moments of fun, joy, and light-heartedness. I experienced success as an athlete and have amazing memories of experiences and adventures. I knew I was loved, but I did not feel deserving.

Nothing is ever truly black and white. I think it is more like river water. Sometimes it is clear and you can see perfectly to the bottom of the riverbed, and other times the sediment has been churned up and you cannot see anything but murky clouds. I believe our lives are like that—sometimes clear and other times messy. This was my reality. I was constantly trying to be happy and was happy and sad, all at the same time. As an adult reflecting on my childhood, I am in awe of how deeply I could feel, how sensitive and aware I was to my world, and by how much emotion my body could hold. It seemed to me that other children might see something and say, "Oh that's sad," perhaps a movie or a real-world event, but I was the child who felt that sadness in my bones, even days later. I felt it all and did not know where to put it. Again, I am in awe of how much work I need to put in as an adult to manage this level of empathy and sensitivity, and as a child, I tried to do this alone.

I recall that the negative self-talk and hurts seemed loudest in the dark when I was a child. Nights were long.

Nighttime was my personal civil war—me against myself. Thoughts, feelings, and memories became too big for my little head and heart to hold. And during the daylight hours, I was just a regular kid too. I know I could have asked for help and my parents would have undoubtedly stepped in, but all I could get out was that I was afraid of the dark.

Mental health was not really something people talked about back then, and that was not even that long ago! You cannot detect a broken psyche, a fractured spirit, or an overloaded emotional heart on an X-ray. It is not until the invisible pain becomes visible that people start to notice and take action. I believe people around me at school suspected I struggled. I also believe that it was easier to dismiss me as a child seeking attention or who was just spoiled and ungrateful rather than see me as a child who was hurting. I think people attributed my major derailment in high school to hanging out with the wrong crowd. The reality is that I felt alone for so long in friendships, I did not even notice they were the wrong crowd; I was just thankful to have someone to sit with.

By grade eleven, I had changed high schools and the new wrong crowd was a whole other level of wrong. This time, instead of being a member of the wrong crowd, doing wrong-crowd-type things, I was the target of that crowd. I was the new kid from the city now in the country—I was an outsider. I made an easy target. I experienced a level of bullying and violence that by today's standards would get teenagers and their parents into major trouble. I also experienced teachers gaslighting me as the perpetrator of the aggression, yet I was the only one left bloodied and bruised.

It was me against a school. That school won that round. As the principal walked me off-site and I was officially expelled, they commented that in all their career in teaching they never saw a student so hated by classmates and teachers alike. I spent the next two weeks in an adult psychiatric hospital.

Yet, despite everything that had happened up to this point, and despite actually being an outsider, and despite the deep emotional pain that was not relieved by my drug use and self-harm, I came upon a truth about myself in that hospital. I could outlast pain. I was a fighter. I could take a hit and stay in the fight. I was still here. I had a lot of broken things, but I was also strong. I had parents who would stand by me. I had parents who would storm heaven with prayers, offer support, and do whatever it took to help me find my way. They were not giving up on me. I had a home team that would never forsake me.

While I was in the hospital, my mom brought me the new Alanis Morissette CD, *Jagged Little Pill*. It had just been released, and Alanis's songwriting was like a balm for my weary heart. During that same visit, my mom challenged me. "I need you to see yourself, Robyne, as I see you. I know you don't see it right now, but you will. You will have a future. You are loved. You are here for a reason. You matter. You have a lot of work to do, but you won't have to do it alone. We are here with you, no matter what. Robyne does hard things. And you also have an army of angels looking after you."

These words from my mom and my own reflection about my capacity to outlast pain ricocheted around my head and heart. I leaned into my mother's words and chose to believe them. My soul thirsted for this positivity, optimism, and strength. Although she had been telling me this for my whole life, the clouds lifted just long enough for me to hear her. I made the commitment to get better. I was going to start over. I was going to accept help. I was going to make a future.

Only a few short weeks later, this quest of reclaiming my life was put to the test. And the words "I can do hard things" changed everything. Let me tell you how.

The accident happened when I was sixteen years old. I was just weeks into my recovery. Although my prior years had been dark, I was trying. I was asking for help. I was working alongside my family to build that once-elusive future I never thought I could catch.

In the darkest hours of February 7, 1996, I found myself clinging to the edge of the ice of the Otonabee River. I had been driving home late one night as a blizzard rolled in. My family had moved north from the Toronto area, which was why I was in a new high school. My driver's licence was weeks old, and the road conditions were treacherous for any driver.

The glow of my headlights was bouncing off walls of snow when I heard a loud bang and felt the dirt from my floor mat hit my face. Moments later, I felt my vehicle being swept away by a mighty force that my brain could not process. And then a sudden and aggressive wave of water struck my face and engulfed the vehicle in mere moments. I took one last gasp of air as my vehicle became a watery tomb. The cold water pierced every part of my body. Soon it began to seep into my lungs. They burned. I wished my body would surrender quickly.

My vehicle had gone off the road, over an embankment, broken through the ice, and crashed into the water. I was trapped in a sinking car under the ice, off a deserted road.

My thoughts did not linger with fear of the situation; rather, I embraced the thought of my mother. I still recall feeling deeply saddened that we were going to be apart. I did not want to die like this. I did not want my parents to live the rest of their lives imagining that their daughter's last moments on earth were the fear and pain of drowning. In that moment, I recalled how my mom used to say, "Robyne can get herself out of anything—homework, chores, and even difficult situations. Robyne is a problem solver. Robyne can do hard things."

My mind made a decision and my heart followed suit. I was going to try to live.

Step 1: *Get out of the seat belt: I wiggled myself out.*

Step 2: *Get out through the window: I escaped through the driver's window.*

Step 3: *Get to the surface of the water . . .*

The water was completely black, and my vision was blurry. I could not tell which way was up. The headlights cast light on the most eerie and frightful scene of what appeared to be a never-ending sea of green water peppered with debris and sediment. I was completely disoriented in the deep, dark, frigid waters. The vehicle was being pulled downstream and sinking with each passing second. I used the last of my energy to focus inward, to quiet my mind. I made the decision to let the final drops of air slip through my lips. I decided to follow the bubbles. I knew they would rise in the water, and I could follow them to the surface.

When I reached what I thought was the surface, I felt ice, and at the same time, waves of exhaustion pulling me down. The current was too strong. It was pulling me aggressively downstream, dragging me under the ice, just below the surface. My winter coat and boots felt like they were cast in cement. My body was fighting the edges of despair, and once again part of me wished to surrender and make this end. But I also knew I just had to get to the edge. Just one thought at a time. Step by step, I was trying to survive each moment. I scrambled to grab the edge of the ice and felt the flesh of my palms being torn as the ice ripped through my frozen skin. I gasped my first breath of air—a million razor blades tearing my lungs apart. Every cell throbbed with exertion and screamed in pain. I recall a nagging feeling of sleep taking over me. All I could see were waves of frigid water rippling over the ice. Loud cracking sounds seemed to suggest the ice was about to let go.

Then I heard it—a faint sound coming from the darkness. Someone was out there! My mind was screaming to that faint voice, but no sound escaped my lips. Finally, I heard his voice: "Help is on the way. I am Joseph." A man had seen my car in the water, stopped, and stepped out onto the chilly riverbank to save me.

Believing in my bones that I can do hard things changed my life. After my accident, I made the decision to keep fighting and create a healthier self. The voice inside that doubted and held me back for years was replaced that night with the steadfast belief that I could do hard things. To this day, that phrase, "I can do hard things," permeates every cell in my body.

Life is hard. Recovery and getting help are hard. Loving and forgiving yourself is hard. Thankfully, we all can do hard things.

I believe one of the biggest barriers to asking for help is the stigma that persists around mental health in our society. Despite my proximity to loving and capable parents, I suffered throughout my childhood in silence. I did not know how to ask for help. In Part II of this book, I'll dive deep into stigma as one of the barriers to resiliency, but for now let me say that stigma is a social cancer. It is also multifaceted. In my experience, the stigma of getting help differs from the stigma that I used to carry with me into my recovery. I felt stigmatized as someone who had experienced mental health episodes. I felt branded as someone who became broken in her childhood and adolescence and was therefore an unlikely candidate for a healthy future. I felt like a time bomb—at any moment, whatever I built could explode and be lost. As I started the process of healing, I felt like an imposter in my own life. I did not know what healthy felt like. I did not know how to be kind to myself. A lot has happened since my teenage years. The dance of recovery is steps forward, back, to the left, and now to the right, and then the tempo changes, and you have to relearn your new way of living over again. No recovery is straightforward. We need to be cognitively nimble to adapt and shift to the ever-changing landscape of what we need in order to be well. With this approach to flexible thinking and an open heart to shifting and adapting to challenge and change, I was able to firmly grasp the once-elusive future and make it my own. I am very much the person I was back then, but I am a better version of myself. The dark days of adolescence are behind me, yet I keep the miracle of my rescue close to my heart. I was given a second chance at life that night.

I still wrestled with negative thoughts years into my recovery. My mindset in childhood and into adolescence was on a self-destructive loop, but I learned how to recognize the patterns. For years, when life got too stressful, unpredictable, and scary, my first thoughts went to a very dark place. This dark place felt real and safe—it was where I spent so much of my time as a child. And I had to retrain my brain not to go there: I had to develop a script to meet the negative thoughts. My new script radiated self-compassion, strength, and a commitment to keep working—to stay in the race. Each time those negative thoughts hijacked my brain, I acknowledged them. I recognized that I used to think like this, that these types of thoughts served a purpose once in my life, but I didn't need them now. I told myself that way of thinking no longer served me; it had helped me then, but I had moved on. I was okay now. I would meet those thoughts without judgement or pressure. I would invite myself to envision another approach that was rooted in self-care, love, compassion, and body kindness—and a deep commitment to keep going. Rest but don't quit.

I believe deeply that our truest self is revealed in moments when we can either give up or get up. These moments shape our authentic capacity to be resilient. I have experienced significant heartbreak and disappointment since my accident— new beginnings are not always smooth. But knowing that I can overcome insurmountable obstacles is part of who I am now. I also believe that our parents' voices and lessons can guide us in our darkest hours. No child or adult is too far gone.

Today, I live my true vocation: mother, wife, educator, practitioner, and emerging author. I am living a life of service to others. It was definitely not a linear route after my accident. It has taken mercy, work, faith, and fortitude. Our lives can be truly transformed when we let go of the shame of our past and meet our authentic self with compassion and forgiveness, recognizing the Herculean strength it takes to say, "I need help," get that help, and then go on to live another day. We cannot hate ourselves healthy. I tried. It didn't work.

It is not lost on me that the institution that contributed so greatly to my troubles is how I was able to find and build my future. With the help of correspondence and a new school, I was able to finish high school on time despite missing a semester. I later went on to finish diplomas and degrees from St. Lawrence College, and Trent, Queen's, and Western universities. That one old high school may have won one round, but I like to think I won the fight!

"Being challenged
in life is inevitable;
being defeated
is optional."

ROGER CRAWFORD

Education is not one school or teacher. It does not have to, nor should it, stay within the bricks and mortar of an academic system or school. Education is learning in motion—being a student of life, meeting new challenges with curiosity and an inquisitive mind. My healing and growth have come from living an examined life. When patterns emerge, I stop and reflect: What lessons should I be learning from these experiences? What do I know and not know about this? How do I get closer to a truth? With self-compassion, humility, and an open head and heart, we can move on, grow, and let go.

I live and work in Peterborough, Ontario, which borders the banks of the Otonabee River, the very river that almost took my life (but also allowed me to take it back). I have a profound appreciation for nature and the power it holds to hurt and to heal.

The man who rescued me that night was awarded the Governor General's Medal of Bravery for rescuing a stranger. Each day I acknowledge that my life is possible because Joseph was sent there and I was rescued. My heart is full of gratitude for his courage. I am also humbled by his lack of judgement of me. Joseph did not know if I was someone who was worthy of his bravery or who deserved rescuing. He put the need of a stranger above his own safety.

It is possible to move to a place where we are no longer alone or held back by the opinions, biases, and discrimination of others who have not yet learned differently. We are part of a community of everyday warriors, showing up and doing the best we can. Maya Angelou wrote, "Do the best you can until you know better. Then when you know better, do better." [2] I lovingly accept that adolescent Robyne was doing the best she could. Now that I know more, I am doing even better.

Each of us matters; we are worthy simply because we are citizens of our planet. I am here as a gentle reminder that our lives are not defined by the broken parts. Maybe those parts of us are not actually even broken in the first place. Failure or mistakes are events, not people.

For some, having their story written by others may serve them. Perhaps the world says, "You are brave, smart, and strong." You internalize this message and it motivates you. Like a storm that is blocking the light, our darkness can seem too difficult to get through, but the light still exists even when we cannot see it. My future was there all along, I just had to fight for it.

No act of bravery should ever be forgotten, and it comes in so many forms. Sometimes, the bravest thing you can do is make the decision to forgive yourself and let go of stigma and destructive self-narratives. There is absolutely no future in your past. Resiliency is in the present. It is available to you in this very moment. You are okay in this moment and you will be okay tomorrow too.

Please stop telling me
I'm not doing it right.

CHAPTER 2

RESILIENCY REDEFINED

RESILIENCY HAS ALWAYS EXISTED. We see resiliency in nature—look how our planet can heal herself. We see resiliency in animals—look at how camels have adapted; see how emperor penguins survive their harsh Antarctic environment. We see resiliency in humanity—we are capable of adapting, evolving, and rising again after countless batterings. Humans have been talking about resiliency in its many forms since at least as far back as the great philosophers. "On pain: If it is unbearable, it carries us off; if it persists, it can be endured," said Marcus Aurelius.[1] And Seneca: "Throw me to the wolves, I will return leading the pack."[2] But interestingly, psychology has not been studying resiliency for as long as many may think. We actually owe the field of resiliency research to our veterans.

Traditionally, the fields of psychology and psychiatry focused on major mental health conditions, both chronic and episodic, that prevented people from participating in normal life. They also tended to take a negative perspective. After the Second World War, when veterans returned home, psychology changed dramatically, expanding to include new ideas about support and services. At the same time, veterans dramatically changed the fields of psychology by becoming psychologists themselves.[3] They brought with them vast knowledge of and insight into the human condition, as well as an ability to develop programming and training. This was because the military had a deep capacity for designing, delivering, and implementing training to large groups of people from diverse backgrounds. Interestingly, it was a veteran-turned-psychologist who implemented group therapy and outpatient treatment programs. These programs, called "mental hygiene clinics," supported people with mental health conditions within their community, rather than institutionalizing them and removing them from society.

It was also around this time that the funding for psychological research shifted. Researchers were now funded to study not only the negatives of mental health, but also the positives. Psychology began to distance itself from the medical model of problem-focused research. The former president of the American Psychological Association, Martin Seligman, is credited with starting the positive psychology movement in 1998. The goals of positive psychology were to focus on a strengths-based model versus the traditional deficit models and to build this knowledge into programs that supported personal development as opposed to repairing problems or weakness.[4]

This is when the seeds of resiliency research as we understand it today took hold. It was no longer a topic or area of

"One who gains strength by overcoming obstacles possesses the only strength which can overcome adversity."

ALBERT SCHWEITZER

research solely for soldiers—the idea of resiliency expanded to include people more generally. The focus shifted from labelling what breaks a person to identifying what makes them thrive through adversity. We know that humans would have had to demonstrate enormous amounts of resiliency to evolve and survive. However, the research on resiliency is really only in its infancy.

Now, I will lay the foundation for my approach to resiliency. Building on the lessons learned from many different approaches and scholars, I position resiliency within the realm of personal discovery and self-actualization. To demonstrate this positioning, let me shine some light on why we all feel like we are not resilient *enough*. Why do we feel as though we are not well equipped to deal with life? Why does life hurt so much? Short answer: life hurts because it is hard. And it is not because you are doing it wrong! Long answer: society and social comparison make life feel this hard. They create gaps or disconnects between who we are, who we think we are, and who we are capable of becoming.

RESILIENCY REDEFINED

Just so we are all on the same page, I want to define resiliency. Resiliency is the capacity to bounce back and rally from adversity. And more importantly, it is how we see ourselves as capable of doing hard things. To me, resiliency is also the practice of taking the broken parts and creating something new, an ability that may not have been open to us had we not gone through hard times. Resiliency is the practice of moving through to get to the other side. It is making the next right decision.

I have had the privilege of working with my collective model of resiliency for several years. Unlike traditional research that packages theories into research programs in the confines of universities or is hidden in academic journals or texts, I wanted my work to be as accessible and broadly available as possible. I wanted these ideas to be shared like stories. I have spoken with people all around the world about my model. The measure of my model's impact is in the sharing of tears, smiles, head nods, high fives, and hugs. It is in strangers telling me that I have come upon something that has awoken part of their soul. It rings with universal truth. At first it was predominantly educators with whom I shared and who I learned alongside, but soon it expanded to front-line workers, health and safety professionals, first responders, military personnel, members of the medical community, athletes, and then into the corporate world. I have been humbled by equal responses coming from small groups to organizational giants. I am excited to share this model with you here formally for the first time in print. This is not intended to be an academic recalling of all things resiliency. It is a story. And I wrote this story for you.

THE BLAST RADIUS OF SOCIAL COMPARISON

I have the privilege of working with people from all corners of the world, in a plethora of settings. What I often hear is that people are exhausted from all the pressures around them. People feel constantly judged. The reality is that people *are* judging you. That is real. You are not imagining it. People are judging other people at an alarming rate. Criticism and commenting have become an acceptable form of communication. I believe that all this judgement is a coping strategy people adopt. People lash out, and they usually lash out at strangers or "others" because they are not coping in their own lives. It is a stress behaviour that becomes misbehaviour. Judgers purposely point out everything and anything they can about other people. Interestingly, what most critical people do not realize is that the criticism of others is actually directed at a hidden part of themselves. The brilliant Carl Jung, the Swiss psychiatrist and psychoanalyst, who also happened to be one of Sigmund Freud's colleagues, explained that seeing others' faults reminds people of their own. He argued that criticizing others alleviates the personal pain people secretly carry about themselves, of not being good enough, so they attack other people. The blast radius of other people's pain is wide and deep. Often, we get caught in its wake.

There are so many examples of external pressures or expectations that people can latch onto as a means of social comparison or social morality. Just look at social media, the constant highlight reel of how we should be living our lives, with all of the comments that flow freely and uncensored. Social media is a breeding ground for the practice of comparing, commenting, and misguided righteousness. The entire system is based on "likes" and approval. Cancel culture demonstrates this in action. Cancel culture is a social media–born trend that decides as a society we should "cancel" someone because of their behaviour. In many cases the behaviour is a recent mistake someone has made; however, in other cases it is a mistake someone made perhaps years ago that has resurfaced. This is a breeding ground of toxicity. My concern with cancel culture is that it has a significant impact on people's lives when context is not always considered. Former president Barack Obama captured this during his speech at the Illinois Institute of Technology on October 29, 2019.

He expressed his concern that we have an overly simplistic world view that a person is no better than their worst choice. He explained: "This idea of purity, and you're never compromised, and you're politically woke, and all that stuff—you should get over that quickly... The world is messy. There are ambiguities. People who do really good stuff have flaws." [5]

When we engage in social comparison behaviours, we rarely perceive ourselves as equal to the people we are looking at—they are either above or below us. In psychology, we call this upward or downward social comparison. We look upward and see people who are more successful, and we feel envy and frustration. We look downward and see people not doing as well as we are, so we feel more successful or better about ourselves. Research explains that this focus on external scripts and expectations is why people are stuck in a constant loop of comparison, criticism, and judgement. This loop increases self-loathing and personal anger, which becomes outward anger. Research also demonstrates that the loop contributes to significant decreases in compassion and empathy. In light of this, our understanding of our own capacity for resiliency and how we connect with others is impacted.

Why Do We Engage in Social Comparison If It Hurts Us?

Rarely do people say that they feel better after spending hours engaged in social comparison. Research supports this as well. A 2014 study explains that social comparison, social media, and self-esteem are all related. The lower the self-esteem, the more screen time engaged in upward social comparison. [6] This means that people who are feeling down look for examples of people who they perceive as doing better than they are, as a means of keeping themselves down. Why would we do this to ourselves? When did social comparison, judging our worth based on others, become so rampant and normative?

The truth is that sometimes we can be our own worst enemy. We can hurt ourselves deeply. When I am working with my students, I explain this behaviour as "personal sliming." We purposefully look at material that hurts us as a form of self-punishment. I believe people do this because they are hurting deeply on the inside and do not really know why. We are in a crisis of disconnection. People want to know why they feel so bad, so they start looking at things that they know hurt them. The pain they feel on the inside is thus matched with an instigator. This makes the hurt make sense. While the effects can seem outwardly harmful (e.g., name-calling, "cancelling" someone), it is actually a form of self-harm, and it is profoundly impacting our capacity to be resilient. We think everyone else is doing life better than we are or that everyone else knows the right way to be resilient. This is not the case.

Where Do We Find Answers?

People are feeling so disconnected, lost, overwhelmed, and really just so far away from the person they want to be. As I said, we are living in a crisis of disconnection when we are supposed to be more connected than ever—instead, we feel abandoned. In a brave attempt to improve this sense of not being okay, people seek copious amounts of information about self-improvement. They seek refuge in personal development materials like self-help books, courses, retreats, and websites. They see and believe that life is supposed to be so much better than this, so they conclude it is their fault. They then seek out plans or strategies to make life better or to get better at living. I hear these ideas when working with people:

"I just have to get [smarter/fitter/healthier/faster/richer/on the right diet], and then I will feel better."

Unfortunately, in the hopes of finding solutions to this personal hurt and sadness, which many people carry daily, some turn to things that could be contributing even more to the problem. Many self-help books are telling people there is something fundamentally wrong with them. This reinforces the belief that they are the problem. So, some self-help books might not be as helpful as we hoped.

The harsh tone of many self-help books seems to start with the notion of getting meaner, grittier, and harder. Mental toughness and elite human performance are the current waves in self-improvement. We have moved away from "just do this" to "just *try* to do this" self-help—meaning that only a few people will actually succeed at following that harsh diet or exercise routine. There are always elusive standards, proclaimed to be reserved for the people willing and capable of doing life right. We are inundated with stories of people presenting themselves as ultra-humans who can take control of their lives, who feel no pain and are now perfect. Perhaps their success is presented as the right food choices, fitness programs, minimalism, early retirement, and Zen-level Stoicism in all situations. On the outside, you are left feeling like they are somehow better equipped to live life right, always. They present a recipe for self-improvement perfection. Or we have book titles that scream obscenities at us as a means of motivation. We have two options: elite athlete or apathetic jerk. It feels like marketing's mission is to break us down and rob us of our basic human right to feel okay. This is helpful for consumerism but hurts us as a society. We buy more when we are down. We are bombarded with messages that we are not good enough. Again, we are left in a state of feeling lack.

Even in the literature on growth mindset created by Carol Dweck, which is widely accepted as positive and helpful, we see, "You're not good enough *yet!*"

Although we live with an abundance of privilege, our emotional health is being heavily taxed and tested. This harsh tone in self-help may work for some, but I am tired of people telling me I am not doing it right or I am not tough enough or angry enough. Rest assured, I know I am tough. I can do hard things. I have done the "don't be sad, be mad" approach. It helped for a time, but there was something missing and I did not feel authentic getting louder. I felt stronger when I became calmer.

People are hurting and are seeking answers. All of the pressures of social comparison and unattainable approaches to self-improvement have resulted in a new age of worry. We are considered the most medically advanced and educated society in history. We should feel safe, but many of us live with this undercurrent of worry. We have access to abundance but feel the edges of scarcity. In the vein of Bruce Springsteen's song "57 Channels (And Nothin' On)," we've got thousands (if not millions) of shows on the stations, but nothing is on. And nothing fills the void. Anxiety, depression, fractured self-esteem, poor relationships, and addictions are on the rise while the markers of wellness are decreasing. We have more than ever, but we feel like we cannot ever catch up to what really matters. We are desperately trying to fill that sense of emptiness and incompleteness. Happiness and wellness feel elusive.

I see people who are tired, disheartened, and discouraged. I talk with people who are sick and tired of feeling sick and tired. I believe there is a real remedy to combat this nagging feeling that something is wrong. The remedy is looking inward, not outward; it is looking forward, not backward. We will never have enough of what we do not need. Viktor Frankl summed this up when he said, "Ever more people today have the means to live, but no meaning to live for."[7]

The Invitation

The answers you seek to some of the greatest questions in your life are not actually in books. They are in you. I think of books and ideas as mirrors. They help us see truth. They help us learn about ourselves by showing us new ways of seeing the world. Books spark an awakening. Your soul recognizes a truth that it needs; that truth is like a balm that soothes and provides relief. But, ultimately, the capacity to experience life differently lies within you. You know yourself better than anyone else on this planet. You are your own expert and you will know what you need. You will know what is true for you. Nothing has worked thus far for many people because it has all been outward-focused. Ideas are being presented as ideals and norms, and we are trying desperately to mimic other people, but those changes do not last. You will never make a change and maintain it if the change is not really you.

The goal here is not to tell you what you are not doing right, but to help you align yourself with a personal practice of resiliency that will in turn help you best navigate your life as you see fit. I want this book to serve as a mirror to help you see what works best for your personal, unique, and authentic practice of everyday resiliency. I want this book to awaken that deep knowledge. What I can offer to you here is a safe place to rest. I invite you to come with me as I share what I have come upon that can protect you from all that noise in society that tells you, *you are not doing it right.*

You already are enough. You have resiliency within you. Now is the time to bring it to the surface.

So, let us start a movement of weary hearts who want deeper meaning and self-acceptance. Let us stop chasing "enough" and finally accept that we already are enough. Learning to stop chasing is a lofty goal, but I also think there is a practical and realistic way of finding this balance. I invite you to think about striving versus chasing—working toward authentic self-acceptance and consistent purposefulness so you feel comfortable in your own skin for a change. The practice to get there is everyday resiliency.

I am not going to tell you what you are doing wrong. I will show you what you are already doing right.

THE BIG IDEAS OF PART I

At the beginning of Part I, I candidly shared the part of my personal story that led me to study resiliency. For many people there is a major critical event or experience that starts a ripple effect of change across their lives. A phone call can change everything. A diagnosis puts you on a future course you never envisioned. A loss leaves your heart irrevocably broken. A sucker punch knocks out your best-laid plans. This is the reality for many—they can point to a moment in time when their lives changed permanently. And for others, it is an invisible, slow, steady erosion that steals their future. It saps their energy, drive, and motivation. One day you realize you are living a life you never asked for. Maybe you feel like a stranger in your own life.

It's like the boiling frog fable: if you put a frog in a pot of boiling water, the frog will jump out immediately. But if you put the frog in the pot of water and bring it to a boil gradually, the frog will boil to death. As we navigate our lives, sometimes we take an immediate hit, and other times, there is a slow leak. Both can bring down a ship.

I know you have a story too. We are all carrying something. Perhaps it is in the past, or maybe you are living it right now. What brings us together is our ability to persist. It is our innate human capacity to be resilient.

At any given moment, we can have a curveball thrown at us that we didn't see coming. It can be big or small. I do not believe we should ever compare hurt, loss, or trauma—each one of us experiences life in our own unique way. The reality is that life hurts sometimes; everyday life is hard, unpredictable, and uncertain. We need to be able to adapt and adjust so that not every setback derails us from what really matters. Poet JmStorm sums this up brilliantly: "It's not good enough to believe in yourself. You have to believe in your failures and understand they have a purpose too."[8]

You've Got This

As you now know, my approach to resiliency is a tender conversation that recognizes that all you will need for this adventure already lies within you. We are born with head and heart alignment—a sense of wholeness, completeness, and self-preservation. That is the root of our survival instincts. A baby does not question whether she deserves food, love, or touch. She intuitively knows she needs it to survive, and she goes after it. In reverse: as a parent I would not rescue one of my children only if they "deserved" to be rescued. Imagine I see Jaxson hanging from a fence, calling for help, but before I go and help him out of the predicament, I wonder if he has

"Experience and success don't give you easy passage through the middle space of struggle. They only grant you a little grace, a grace that whispers, 'This is part of the process. Stay the course.'"

BRENÉ BROWN

cleaned his room. Of course, I would not measure Jaxson's need for assistance and help him based on his performance! Typically, in situations such as these, our instincts know better and take over. We intuitively help, because our behaviours and performance should not equal our worth or value.

While our natural instinct is to protect ourselves, we are disconnected from this primal drive that knows we are enough as we are. The layers of life and our relationship with ourselves cause friction between the head and heart. How many times do you know something to be true in your head, but find your heart wants a different outcome? You may know something intellectually, but your body feels it differently. You can lessen this divide between the head and heart through alignment. It takes work, but you can once again get on the same page intellectually and emotionally. To do so, let's first explore what creates this separation.

Many people I work with recall that they were conditioned early on in their lives to create the distance between their head and their heart. They were trained to believe that emotions are a weakness and our thoughts or intellect matter more. Perhaps you were told to "take the emotion out of it" or not to get too angry. Or you were led to believe that good children keep their emotions in check. In childhood, these norms are presented both explicitly and implicitly. We then internalize our compliance with these norms as a measure of worthiness or goodness. We are taught and conditioned how our thoughts, feelings, and behaviours are to fit. The most common message I heard from the outside world was this: "Life would be so much easier, Robyne, if you weren't so sensitive and emotional, and if you didn't take everything so personally or to heart!" Or they blamed my temper on my red hair. Classic! If you can keep this delta between your heart and head in adulthood, you are likely to be mislabelled a true professional! And then you will spend years of your adulthood desperately trying to feel anything again. Eventually the feelings will stop, if we ignore them long enough, and then we will miss them dearly. I have worked with top business leaders who share that they just want to feel again. They spent so much time in their head, their heart feels numb.

It is hard to carry the weight of your life and world with just two hands. I am here to share research-informed *wise* practices, not best practices, that will guide you toward personal alignment—having your head and heart finally on the same page. The notion of wise practices came from a dear colleague who studies Indigenous ways of knowing. She explained to me that "wise" here means learned through experience, while "best" is a Western idea of superiority or hierarchy. I choose to use the term "wise practices" here rather than "best practices" because this is not a practice of good, better, best. It is honouring our personal experiences and connecting to the wisdom of learning from our mistakes.

Because of life experiences, deep hurts, and emotional setbacks, many of us lose touch with the importance of listening to our instincts, practicing self-preservation, and knowing we are enough. We are hurting from our pasts; we are running a race with no finish line; we are exhausted by the obligatory; and we are holding on to practices that do not serve us. We are working ourselves to death instead of working ourselves into more life. It does not have to be this way.

Fostering a sense of enough is possible for all of us. What you have done up to this point only equips you even more to know what you want and do not want in life. Rest assured your future is about your hunger, not your history.

To start us on the path of adopting a new approach to resiliency, I will describe the barriers. What gets in the way?

From my work across many platforms and working with people from diverse backgrounds, I have observed that there are three common elements that impede our quality of life and our performance: stress, fear, and stigma. As Seneca wrote, "We suffer more in our imagination than in reality."[9] Although we know the stress, fear, and stigma are real, how we suffer from them is in our minds, bodies, and souls. It is not imagined, but it is invisible. We need to shine a light on these shadows. We need to make the invisible visible so we can address these obstacles head-on. So, let us examine the barriers to resiliency so we can chart a new course.

PART II

— THE —

THREE

OBSTACLES

"

I finally accepted that I could not calm the storm, but I could calm myself, and the storm did pass.

"

CHAPTER 3

STRESS

SPRING BREAK IS approaching and the students at the local elementary school can almost taste it. My friend, a seasoned teacher who has shepherded thousands of children from elementary to high school over his thirty-year career, stands with a heavy heart, worried mind, and forced smile. He knows some of his students will experience summer camps, family vacations, sports and arts programs. They will have all sorts of glorious memory-making moments. And he also knows that some students, in the very same class, will experience food shortages, abuse, neglect, isolation, and real fear. For these children, leaving school for the summer means they will not have contact with the only caring and responsible adult they know. These students have to go through the motions of showing their classmates that they are also excited about the eight-week break from school. If not, their truths and reality might become known to the children who live in privilege. These children who live in a stark reality of oppression and disadvantage have learned how to hide their realities. They know how to armour up and protect themselves, and even how to protect the very families who are hurting them. This teacher knows first-hand what stress does to children and their families. He repeats this routine every school holiday, PD day, and summer vacation.

One student confides in the teacher that he is so worried he might forget some of the algebraic formulas and is nearly in tears begging for more homework so he can get ahead and stay ahead. This student feels stress, and that stress is real.

Another student confesses that he is stressed that he may not be able to protect his sister this summer from Children's Services. He is worried that he will be separated from his siblings since he is turning thirteen years old. His stress is real.

The final bell rings and the students disperse. The teacher will carry those children in his heart all summer as he has done for twenty-nine other summer holidays. His stress is real too.

For us to understand resiliency and how people can keep showing up in their lives despite the varying and deeply personal hardships, we need to understand the common obstacles—the stuff that gets in the way and knocks us down. There are obviously more than three obstacles that any one of us could face on any given day; however, in my work, I consistently come upon three: stress, fear, and stigma. These three barriers get in our way, but they can also hold us back. Despite our best-laid plans, once we experience stress, fear, and stigma, our ability to maintain our sense of self is deeply challenged and our resiliency decreases.

WHAT IS STRESS?

I am sure you have heard about stress. I am pretty sure you may have also heard that stress is going to kill us. It is known as the silent killer of the twenty-first century. We see reports with titles such as, "Stress Is Linked to 80 Per Cent of All Medical Illnesses" or headlines like, "Best to Not Stress the Small Stuff, Because It Could Kill You" or "Stress: The Killer Disease." These headlines run in reputable magazines and journals. It is a common message across the board. Stress is bad. Stress is going to kill us.

It used to be margarine. I remember when in the '80s margarine was going to kill us. I recall going to people's houses and seeing margarine in the refrigerators and thinking, "Wow, no one told them. Margarine is going to wipe out this whole family." This idea of the harmful effects of margarine came from a documentary I watched when I was little, and this experience created a real sense of danger.

I wonder how children today must feel when they hear us talk about stress. I suspect, and have seen first-hand, that children are terrified, just like I was, but this time it is not about one product like margarine—it is everywhere. I would also argue that most children have heard about how bad stress is more than once in their lifetime. Even though science has debunked the claim that margarine kills, my food fear lingers—and again, that was after one episode of exposure. I reflect sometimes on why children of today would ever want to grow up. We are not painting an attractive picture of adulthood, and we are passing along an extremely fractured and volatile world. Our planet is suffering. There is brutality in our streets. People are cruel. Social justice issues are rampant, and we seem to be more divided than ever. And it is not just

"In order to realize the worth of the anchor we need to feel the stress of the storm."

CORRIE TEN BOOM

the outside world. Families and individuals are experiencing very high levels of stress and fear.

Moreover, family systems are stretched, and people are weary. According to Statistics Canada, one in four adults report living in daily extreme stress. In the same study, 62 per cent reported that their greatest stressor was work and time away from family, a result of working outside the home.[1] Children are being raised in an ecosystem of stress that is coming at them from every angle—from school, society, and families.

Recent global events have exasperated an already fragile system. This was evident when we found ourselves in a global health pandemic with COVID-19. The first half of 2020 walloped us. People across the planet struggled and continue to struggle in their own way. I believe that the events of 2020 will be taught in future history classes. We are all knowledge holders of what this experience has been like to live through. As global citizens, we were at first instructed to shelter in place. For some this meant trying to work from home, and/or navigating elder care or raising and teaching children out of school, and for others, sheltering in place brought total isolation from everyone and everything. Grocery shopping required people to learn new protocols. Loved ones were separated. Many people died. We all collectively grieved our illusions of certainty and predictability, the semblance of normal life, events that had been planned, now cancelled. Stress was rampant. Then, as the global pandemic was going into its sixth month, a needed racial reckoning swept through North America. An already weary world was now faced with another reality that rocked many of us to our core. I feel as though the world was scorched to the ground, leaving her mark on our mental and emotional health.

I once visited a classroom and a young student pulled me aside. He was about eight or nine years old, and he asked me if I had heard of climate change. I replied that I had heard about global warming and that it is a serious issue. "Mother Earth is hurting," I said to him. He asked me if I had heard that his generation was going to fix it. I let him know that I had, and that I also believed wholeheartedly that the future generation would be eco-stewards of the lands and make a difference. He looked at me, puzzled and afraid. "Don't count on us!" he said. "We have no idea how to do this. Besides, I'm not even allowed to use the toaster when my mom isn't home. How am I going to fix a planet?"

Fair question. How sad that this is causing him so much stress alongside such big feelings of helplessness. We talked more and I showed him pictures on my phone of scientists I know who are not only studying solutions to global warming, but also teaching students, in university, how to think about our environmental issues. I wanted to leave him with the reassurance that he was not alone, that others are also stressing about this—he is part of a greater community who share the load of his worries. Ecological stress and even ecological grief are very real.

Stress is all around us. I think it is imperative that we start learning more about stress and working with a more productive narrative about its effects. We know our daily lives are stress-filled. And at times it feels impossible to change or escape what society has become. The fast-paced rat race of consumerism, rampant narcissism, and a lack of regard for our interconnectedness as humans is all around us. But there is another way.

I love how Sister Joan Chittister, in her book *The Time Is Now: The Call for Uncommon Courage*, shares a deep, bold, and soul-stirring look at the world around us. She explains that when we look around at all the stress and stressors in the world, we need to take action. She encourages us not to get caught up in the "niceties," to combat complacency and apathy in this modern world, rather than wait for others to solve the problems of inequality, injustice, and poverty for us. Chittister argues that it is both our moral and spiritual responsibility to take action ourselves so we can make the world a better place for everyone. There is something pretty amazing about a Benedictine nun taking on the stress-inducing and soul-damning nature of the great establishment! Despite how inescapable our stress-fuelled culture and lives feel, there are ways to experience stress differently.

Let us take a close look at what we can do to foster a different relationship with our stress. Again, my intention with this book is to share research-informed practices with you that are accessible, realistic, and sustainable. There is a lot of information about stress management that seems stressful in itself. Where do you even begin? Before you go and sell off all of your possessions, and move to a cabin in the woods with no Wi-Fi and cases of essential oils and wine, keep reading, not only for your sake but for that of all the children out there too!

Despite how familiar we are with the idea of stress, it is shockingly difficult to define stress clearly. Some researchers define it as a normal biological reaction to potential danger. When you encounter a stressful situation, your brain floods your body with chemicals and hormones. We talk a lot about adrenaline and cortisol in this definition. The Canadian Mental Health Association defines stress more broadly, explaining that stress can be cognitive, emotional, physical, or behavioural.[2] The traditional medical model defines stress as physical, mental, and emotional factors that cause bodily or mental tension. For our purposes, I like to think of stress as the aftermath of our body's internal fire alarm. The alarm signals a batch of hormones and chemicals to call us into action. We must fight, flee, or freeze our way out of the danger zone.

Stress is a full-bodied experience. It can instantly affect how we think, feel, and behave. Stress has no boundaries.

The paradigm shift I want to present here about stress does start by acknowledging and recognizing that stress is a reaction that impacts us on all levels—biologically, physically, emotionally, and spiritually. And it is necessary for our survival and growth. Stress is a necessary part of our humanity. In her book *Untamed*, Glennon Doyle sums this up perfectly: "If you are uncomfortable—in deep pain, angry, yearning, confused—you don't have a problem, you have a life. Being human is not hard because you're doing it wrong, it's hard because you are doing it right. You will never change the fact that being human is hard, so you must change your idea that it was ever supposed to be easy." [3]

Stress is part of the "hard" of life. Accepting this, let's look at what we can now do with this knowledge.

STRESS INCREASES PERFORMANCE

We lose most people in the conversation about stress because all their energy is going toward preventing the stress or trying to get rid of it. We are bombarded with messages that we must get rid of our stress, but the research tells another story.

Do you have a favourite bell curve figure? I sure do. The Yerkes-Dodson Human Performance and Stress Curve from 1908. [4] I remember learning about this as an undergraduate psychology student and was in disbelief that this image was not on cereal boxes and billboards, and did not have its own clothing line. I recall asking my professor why the world didn't talk about this more. People need to know this. Well, dear reader, here you go!

The Yerkes-Dodson Human Performance and Stress Curve

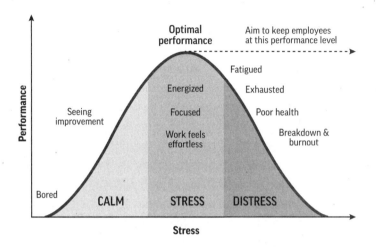

Researchers Robert Yerkes and John Dillingham Dodson discovered the law of performance and stress. Their game-changing work explains that there is an empirical relationship between arousal and performance. The law states that performance increases with physiological or mental arousal, but only up to a point. What this means is that stress (what they called arousal) will actually increase our performance, but only to a particular threshold or point. Once the stress levels get too high, performance will decrease. When there is no stress, performance is lacking. When stress builds, we start seeing improvements. When we are in our peak zone, we experience optimal performance. The work feels energizing and effortless, and we are focused.

When coaching people with this framework, I use the notion that this peak zone is our "A-game." We feel great. We are getting things done. We are proud of ourselves. This can be referred to as eustress or good stress. What is important to note here is that the stress itself is not good or bad. People mistakenly think of good versus bad stress, but really it is how the body is responding to the stress. The stress composition is exactly the same if you are excited about a new job opportunity or if you are being chased by a bear. It is how the body *experiences* the stress that is either positive and productive or excessive and destructive. The key is how the body is responding to the stress in a productive way.

In a positive stress experience, the body responds to a challenging task as it should. The brain's fire alarm has gone off briefly to let us know this work is important, and we experience the chemicals and hormones that help produce fluidity to our work. But this is effective only up to a point. Once we cross the threshold of too much stress, too many tasks or competing demands, our performance starts to decrease. We feel fatigued or exhausted. I see this as the zone of distress, where we make mistakes.

You know you have crossed into the zone of distress when you can't string a sentence together, spell a word, find your keys, or remember basic information. In my case, I start dropping things—physical things like phones, passports, and coffee mugs, but also mental things, too, like who needs to be picked up from where or forgetting to eat or why I walked upstairs.

When we spend too much time in the distress zone, we get sick, feel constantly overwhelmed, and risk burnout. I want to be in the zone of stress. Imagine how strange that would sound in a conversation if I told you that I was desperately trying to stay in a constant state of stress! This is the problem: we talk about stress wrong. We have bought into the idea that stress is the bad guy. But distress is where the errors happen and where we get sick. So, how do we get some more stress?

STRESS REVISITED

We know what it feels like when we are on our A-game. We know when we are balanced. We know what it feels like to have a sense of agency and control. We know when we are ahead in life. I find this idea fascinating: *getting ahead in life*. How do we get ahead in life when we all live in the present moment? This is an unrealistic expectation. We all get one second at a time. We can be only here, in the very moment in which we find ourselves. What I see most often is people either stuck in the past or worrying about the future. This is the distress breeding ground.

I used to think of stress as a full-body reaction to anything in life that I didn't see coming, I didn't understand, I couldn't control, or I couldn't protect myself or my loved ones from. Stress was an external event that manifested as a physical reaction. It was an intruder.

It was only after I started learning about mindfulness that I came upon the idea that my stress was attacking me not only externally but internally as well. Our minds could conjure up stress too: how and what we think about events or tasks create the reaction or initiate the series of biological events. My mind could unleash a civil war—me versus myself. When I realized this, I knew I needed to revisit and redefine my understanding of stress.

Kelly McGonigal's book *The Upside of Stress* is an excellent read for revisiting our understanding of stress. McGonigal does not suggest how to minimize stress but rather how to get better at it. The book starts by sharing results from a groundbreaking study in 2012, conducted by Whitney P. Witt from the University of Wisconsin–Madison, that also changed how McGonigal thought about stress. With more than

29,000 people in their study, the researchers examined how a person's perception of their stress impacted their physical health. Participants rated if their stress levels influenced their health "a little," "a moderate amount," or "a lot." Eight years later, the researchers used public death records to compare to their original sample. In a shocking discovery, people who had reported that their stress impacted their physical health "a lot" had an increased prevalence of death by 43 per cent! Participants who reported that their stress levels impacted their health "a little" were less likely to have died compared to everyone else in the study.[5] What we can learn from this study is that if we believe that our stress is going to kill us, we're probably right. If we believe our stress is not impacting our health, we're also probably right. Telling ourselves that stress is killing us is not helpful; it is damn well harmful.

Another group of researchers, Alia Crum, Peter Salovey, and Shawn Achor, categorized stress in two ways, debilitating or enhancing, and found similar results. Their findings support the idea that the story we tell ourselves about our stress matters.[6] I have included the Stress Mindset Measure here for you to complete.

Stress Mindset Measure (SMM)

This eight-item measure was developed by Crum, Salovey, and Achor to address the extent to which an individual adopts a mindset that the effects of stress are enhancing or debilitating. Items, listed below, evaluate a participant's general stress mindset (e.g., "The effects of stress are negative and should be avoided"), as well as signs and symptoms related to the enhancing and debilitating consequences of stress in the realms of health and vitality, learning and growth, and performance and productivity (e.g., "Experiencing stress improves my health and vitality"). Participants rated items on a five-point scale ranging from 0 = strongly disagree to 4 = strongly agree. SMM scores are obtained by reverse-scoring the four negative items (indicated by an asterisk) and then taking the mean of all eight items. Higher scores on the SMM represent the mindset that stress is enhancing.

Stress Mindset Questions

Rate the extent to which you agree or disagree with the following questions (scoring: use this scale for all eight; the asterisks below indicate reverse scoring).

0 = Strongly Disagree
1 = Disagree
2 = Neither Agree nor Disagree

3 = Agree
4 = Strongly Agree

1 The effects of stress are negative and should be avoided. *

2 Experiencing stress facilitates my learning and growth.

3 Experiencing stress depletes my health and vitality. *

4 Experiencing stress enhances my performance and productivity.

5 Experiencing stress inhibits my learning and growth. *

6 Experiencing stress improves my health and vitality.

7 Experiencing stress debilitates my performance and productivity. *

8 The effects of stress are positive and should be utilized.

This survey is helpful for exploring your ideas about how stress impacts your health. Take a moment to reflect on your answers. Do you believe that stress is bad for you? Do you think stress should be avoided? And most importantly, do you believe that your stress is going to kill you? I invite you to take some time to explore what you hold as truth, and then investigate where those beliefs came from. By understanding your beliefs and their origins, you can start to develop new perspectives and plan a course of belief corrections when the old beliefs come up.

Here is an example. Say your difficult boss gives you an unreasonable task. Your first thought is, "Oh, this is going to be it—this is going to break me. I am fed up with bosses who have no clue how to lead." This response is going to impact your health. How you talk to yourself about that unreasonable task is going to be internalized. These thought patterns are not good for you and that cost is not worth it.

So, alternatively, you could say to yourself, "Wow! Here is another example of how my boss totally does not get my job or know how to lead. I am going to do the best I can to get this done, but ultimately, they do not pay me enough, nor is it worth it to my health and personal peace to internalize this anger and frustration."

In both examples, the boss is unreasonable and probably not a great leader, but you are choosing how to carry this fact. Option A: internalize it and let the anger rob you of your peace. Or Option B: protect your calm and let the bad boss behaviour bounce off your armour that surrounds your peace. Be gentle and patient with yourself here. Belief correction takes practice and commitment. Some days this will be easy: you will be a badass, a warrior, and you will take no garbage. On other days, you will wake yourself up at three in the morning and not be able to get back to sleep because of bad-boss-behaviour frustration.

Thankfully, McGonigal shares more strategies. In her work, which interconnects with that of Crum, Salovey, and Achor, she frames three additional productive beliefs about your stress that are helpful for minimizing its harmful effects:

1 View your body's stress response as helpful, not debilitating or harmful—view stress as energy.

2 View yourself as able to handle, and even learn and grow from, the stress in your life.

3 View stress as something everyone deals with and as a natural part of our humanity.

Each one of us will have a different way of internalizing these beliefs. Some may read them once, have a switch go off in their head, and just know differently from then on. Others may have to write the beliefs down, reread them, or even make Post-it Notes or screen-capture images to constantly remind themselves, for example, "This situation isn't going to kill you." Whatever your case may be, I hope this helps you reframe stress and minimize the needless harm and worry. But don't be too hard on yourself: learning to reframe and revisit stress may take some time. Remember, common sense does not equal common practice. But with intention and commitment, we can start to adopt a new way of thinking and being. We need to be intentional with our thoughts about stress and distress. You may also have to keep reminding yourself and the people around you that stress is not the enemy.

Additionally, you may have to take a stand against the parts of our Western culture that promote stress-living as a sign of accomplishment and success. Burnout, broken families, hurting, and overwhelm are not signs of superior living. So, look at your results of the SMM. How you perceive stress is going to have an impact on how you move forward. Can you incorporate new language about how you talk about your stress? For example, instead of saying, "This stress is going to kill me," you could say, "I am feeling this stress. It is important that I make sure to unwind tonight. With this stress in my body, I need time to regroup and relax." Another way could be saying or thinking, "Stress in, distress out," paired with a few deep breaths. I always liked the phrase, "Inhale confidence and exhale worries." There will always be stress in our days, but those days can be processed in our minds as difficult but not deadly. How we speak about our stress matters. Our bodies are listening.

On a hopeful note, we can take a closer look at a study conducted by Michael Poulin at the University at Buffalo. Poulin and his team interviewed a large sample of participants about their stress levels and their helping behaviours toward others, or what is often referred to as acts of altruism. Interestingly, the researchers found similar results to the other research studies mentioned here—that stress increased the likelihood of mortality by 30 per cent when participants believed stress is harmful. However, Poulin and his team also discovered that when people with high levels of stress also reported high levels of helping behaviour, the health risks were negated. The researchers concluded that being helpful to others significantly reduces stress-related mortality rates.[7] This is a huge finding. Typically, when we are experiencing distress, our natural tendency is to retreat, pull away from others, and focus inward. We think our situation is more challenging than that of other people, and we often "one-up" each other with our difficulties. Distress greatly reduces our compassion and empathy toward others. Considering what the research shows us, when we are hurting or in distress, the goal is to find relief not only in how we talk about stress to ourselves, but also by being of service to others.

Following a talk in the Sudbury area, a woman shared with me that after the loss of her adult son in a workplace accident, she was devastated. She and her family thought she would never bounce back. She said she was so disappointed in how people treated her after her son died, and observed that people do not know what to do or say around someone who is grieving. The woman also shared with me that after several years, she decided she needed to do something about this. She joined a program called Threads of Life (threadsoflife.ca), a non-profit organization that supports families who have lost a loved one in a workplace accident. This organization and those like it provide not only a community for belonging, acceptance, and hope, but also the opportunity to be of service to others. In helping others who were earlier on in their loss and grief journey, she was finally able to start healing too. This woman was able to be the person she said she needed after her son's accident. She could speak the language of loss as only someone who has journeyed that path can. I can only imagine the impact she has had on others. I think of this as the "heavy heart work." And I thank every person who is willing to share their pain and story in true and authentic vulnerability as a means of supporting others. It is in helping others that we can start helping ourselves.

66

Courage doesn't mean you don't get afraid. Courage means you make the conscious decision to not let that fear stop you.

99

CHAPTER 4

FEAR

IN 1973, THE London *Sunday Times* reported about the now classic R. H. Bruskin Associates' American Fear study.[1] The headline read that people feared public speaking more than death! This is a statistic to which many still refer. In 2012, researchers Karen Dwyer and Marlina Davidson even set out to replicate this study and found similar results.[2]

I find this fascinating, since prior to COVID-19 I spent a lot of my time travelling around North America for speaking events. Getting onstage is nothing compared to the fear I feel on the flight to the event, when there is turbulence! That is when I go into full-on fear mode. I have the wildest rituals when I fly to keep that fear monster in her cage. My rational brain knows that turbulence does not cause plane crashes. So I evoke visualization exercises to address my seemingly out-of-control fear reaction during turbulence. I imagine our plane flying in Jell-O. The plane moves aggressively up and down through the storm as I envision a die-cast miniature airplane in Jell-O. The atmosphere fills the space between the plane and the ground. We are in Space Jell-O.

Fear is fear, regardless of what triggers it. But thankfully we can develop tools to keep our fear monsters in their cages. I like to imagine feeding my fear monster Jell-O at the end of each flight.

STRESS AS WE KNOW IT

I used to think of fear and stress in a "you can't have one without the other" kind of way. They are mirroring, interrelated, and enmeshed experiences. However, when you take a closer look, you can see how they are related but different. You can have stress without fear, but you cannot be afraid without stress. Stress is more the kind of biological response that I explained in the previous chapter. Not all stress is fear-related. Preparing for a big event or being excited about a special trip may be stressful but may not trigger fear. Fear is experienced when we feel or interpret impending threat or doom. Stress joins the fear so we can experience full-on emotional arousal as a result of the impending dangers, pain, threat, or harm. It is the *thinking* about danger that sounds off the biological response based on how we are perceiving a situation. Our brain interprets an event or idea, then quickly makes a hypothesis about how threatening it is. If our brain senses potential harm, we feel fear. What is unique about fear is that both real and imagined situations can cause deep fear. Fear is so powerful because it is one of our most primitive human emotions.

I think of it this way: from an evolutionary perspective, those without a strong fear system were probably killed off because they were not alert to the dangers around them. Everyone who is still alive today had ancestors with a strong fear system. These people were the ones at the watering hole making sure the coast was clear before they closed their eyes and took a drink.

Everyone feels fear. Researchers Sylco Hoppenbrouwers, Eric Bulten, and Inti Brazil found that even people with anti-social personality disorder, or those thought of as "psychopaths" ("psychopath" is not an official diagnosis) feel fear. The difference in this group of people is that despite feeling fear, they don't see the danger.[3]

Although fear is universal, how people interpret events is unique and personal. Essentially, fear and excitement are the same emotion! Take public speaking: some consider it one of their most dreaded situations and avoid it at all costs. Others, although the fear system is activated, feel excited! Performer Tania Rose explained her feeling before she takes the stage: "Your heart races, you feel butterflies flapping wildly in your gut, your breathing intensifies, you feel a sense of heightened sensitivity as your eyes widen and your limbs quiver with anticipation. Fear or excitement? It's both. The only difference between fear and excitement is the way you think about it."[4]

The phenomena that Rose described are the result of how the brain interprets the sudden adrenaline rush. We think about it, decide about it, and then experience it as fear or excitement. The adrenaline released is the same either way, but we call it fear or excitement based on our personal preferences. But where do these distinctions come from?

"FEARARCHY"

The feararchy was introduced by Karl Albrecht in 2007. He argued that humans experience five types of fear:

1 **Extinction:** fear of death or dying or no longer being around

2 **Mutilation:** fear of anything happening to our body—this also includes anything invading our body's boundaries

3 **Loss of autonomy:** fear of being immobilized in any form—being in a situation beyond your control

4 **Separation:** fear of abandonment, rejection, or loss

5 **Ego-death:** fear of humiliation, shame, or any other self-disapproval—losing worthiness[5]

All fear fits somewhere on this hierarchy of fear, or feararchy. These are the foundations of fear, but we experience them differently, at different ages. For example, babies are born with two innate fears: fear of falling and fear of loud noises. As we grow, we start taking on more fears, which are both innate and learned.

Most of our fears are greatly impacted by our childhood experiences, environment, and culture. Again, as we age, fear starts to take hold mostly by association. Many of our fears are learned within our family systems; you may even notice some passed down to you by your parents. I heard a fascinating story about a mom who had a deep fear of rejection, stemming from her childhood. This mom lived with constant fear that her son would also have no friends in elementary school. One day, she was watching him play soccer and was overcome by a sudden surge of fear rooted in her perception that her son was being excluded by other kids. She wasn't seeing clearly: she ran up to her son and told him to go and be with the other children. The son, totally embarrassed, explained to his mom that he was the goalie in the soccer game, and he was supposed to stand in the net while the other kids ran up the field! The mom's fear was so great, she couldn't even process that her son was playing soccer. She just reacted out of her own fear of rejection. The scene of other kids running away from her son likely triggered a trauma response she had to children running away from her as a child. The feararchy plays out in our everyday lives in such unexpected ways.

PASSING PARENTAL FEARS

As parents or supporters, we need to keep our fears in check. There are enough fears our children will hear about in the world; we do not need to mindlessly add to a child's list! For me, I had to be careful not to pass my fear of birds on to my children. I know—my name is Robyne and I am afraid of birds! This fear began after an incident when I was in primary school, probably about five or six years old. My school was just down the street from Lake Ontario, and we used to walk there often as a class. On one of our trips, a classmate was near the edge of a small feeder pond next to the lake, and a swan came out of nowhere, flew down, and attacked him. I had never seen a swan fly, let alone attack someone. I remember the boy screaming and fighting back, teachers yelling, feathers and blood everywhere. My teacher later tried to explain that the boy probably got too close to the swan's nest without knowing it. Needless to say, I don't think of swans as romantic or elegant, and I don't much care for birds.

The fear morphed as I aged, and now I feel fear in the presence of all birds—yes, even the cute little chickadees! So, as a parent, I used to tell my kiddos when they were small that mommy was not really on friendly terms with birds, but they could be. My children soon became my bird protectors. They would chase away seagulls or street pigeons and took great pride in the fact that they could do something I could not. Just because you have a fear, does not mean it has to get passed on.

FEAR AS A BARRIER

Imagine how many dreams and goals do not even start because of fear. I believe that fear keeps us from opportunities and living to our fullest potential. Cheryl Strayed said, "Fear, to a great extent, is born of a story we tell ourselves."[6] This idea is so relevant and profound. Fear and how we think about fearful events wreak havoc on our minds and hearts. In Western society it has become relatively common to avoid risks. We avoid anything that can jeopardize certainty or security. People routinely choose comfort over challenge. We choose to play it safe even at the cost of our dreams and talents. Of course, safety is important, but when we are so stuck on always settling and being safe, there is no room to grow.

We are told that it's smart to pursue comfort, ease, and convenience. So many people have adopted this idea. I see this in the university often. "What job will this degree get my child?" "What would they even do with a humanities degree?" It is the idea that concrete, predictable, and stable wins the race in life. Degrees that give you a prescriptive job at the end

"Most human beings only think they want freedom. In truth they yearn for the bondage of social order, rigid laws, materialism. The only freedom man really wants is the freedom to be comfortable."

JOHN TELLER, *SONS OF ANARCHY*

are the only degrees that matter. I disagree wholeheartedly with this belief. Life is so much more than being comfortable and complacent.

Although we are technically wired for safety, security, and social approval, we can still choose to veer outside of our comfort zones. I like to think that the best personal growth and stories come when we venture outside of these zones and take smart risks. We don't grow while we are in our comfort zones. The magic is just outside of it—when we do something that we wished we could and make it happen.

I invite you to think about something that you have done in your life that you are really proud of. Big or small, it doesn't matter. I bet whatever you are most proud of likely needed you to stretch and wasn't easy. That's how life works. We need to be uncomfortable and challenged to really see what we are capable of. We grow when we choose to be brave and face adversity and challenge head-on. If it doesn't challenge you, it won't ever change you. I like Nido Qubein's quote: "Your present circumstances don't determine where you can go; they merely determine where you start."⁷ Where you go is totally up to you. Often, we let fear prevent us from moving forward, but the real adventure is feeling the fear and choosing to do it anyway.

RESILIENCY AND FEAR

Being resilient does not mean you don't feel fear or have moments of being afraid. It is actually in our times of fear that we see our true resiliency. In those moments, we can see what we are truly made of. I think of these lines from George R. R. Martin's book *A Game of Thrones*: "Can a man still be brave if he's afraid?" asks the young boy Bran, to which his father,

Eddard Stark, responds, "That is the only time a man can be brave."[8] Being willing to take the first step toward whatever you are hoping for is true bravery. Being willing to love again after your heart has been broken, or taking the leap of going back to school, or shouldering the risks of starting a business— all will require facing fears. Any life event that is really worth doing will require you to choose to be brave.

I remember my son Hunter's first day of high school. He was fairly nervous, like most teenagers, starting the next chapter of his life. I shared with him lines by writer Benjamin Mee: "You know, sometimes all you need is twenty seconds of insane courage. Just literally twenty seconds of just embarrassing bravery. And I promise you, something great will come of it."[9] I assured Hunter that he wouldn't have to be insanely courageous for four long years of high school. That day, he just needed to be brave enough to walk in the front door.

So, how do we choose bravery when all our body, mind, and heart are screaming for is safety and comfort? Well, thankfully, author and podcaster Tim Ferriss has a solution.

FEAR-SETTING

When I first heard about Ferriss's work on the practice of fear-setting, I was once again asking why on earth it was not in every school curriculum, like the Yerkes-Dodson Human Performance and Stress Curve. Well, apparently, the idea has been around for quite some time, since around 301 BC! What Ferriss did, however, was extraordinary: he was able to shine new light on an ancient philosophical practice and make it accessible for those of us who don't have a philosophy degree.

Ferriss developed a practice of teaching people how to define fears instead of goals.[10] His work is based on the ancient practice of Stoicism, which has been around for more than 2,300 years. In simple terms, Stoicism is a practice for living your life and can be used as a tool to help you think and act in an unpredictable world. I think we could all use help with this! It teaches us how to sort out what we can and cannot control. It helps us choose a direction for our thinking and behaving that can lead us to personal fulfillment. It is based on three main ideas: living in agreement with nature, living by virtues, and knowing what you can control.

Living in agreement with nature means that as rational creatures we should apply our natural ability to reason to all our actions. This is the foundation of being a critical thinker and not being pulled and pushed in competing directions by others. We know what is good for us. We also know what is harmful to us. When we choose things that are harmful to us anyway, simply because "everyone else is doing it," we are not living in agreement with our nature. Someone else is doing the thinking for us. We want to be in alignment with our true nature of being a rational thinker.

Living by virtues means that we make decisions based on the four cardinal virtues: wisdom or prudence, justice or fairness, courage or fortitude, and self-discipline or temperance. We make decisions and act based on the virtues, not on fear or social approval. Any time we are presented with a task, we respond and behave in a manner that reflects our virtues.

Knowing what you can control means you take stock of what is and what is not up to you. What is always up to us are our thoughts, judgements, and actions. What is not up to us is essentially everything else!

So, at this point, you might be wondering what this has to do with fear-setting and resiliency. Here we go.

Ferriss's practice of fear-setting works in three parts. First, you think of the things you want to do but may not be doing because of fear. Write down the thing and then list whatever is fearful about it (*define*). Next to each of the fears, write down how you could *prevent* it from happening. Lastly, write down how you would *repair* each situation if the worst happened. The next step is to explore what the cost is of not doing each thing. Explore inaction. If you choose not to do that thing, what would it cost you personally, emotionally, physically, socially, or spiritually (*cost of inaction*)?

The last step is exploring what could happen if you did your thing or even partially did it. What is the potential outcome? What could happen? What could go right (*benefits*)?

Let's walk through two examples. Say I'm thinking I might want to write a book and maybe also run another half-marathon. Good grief, those are both fear-evoking thoughts!

The Things
1) Write a book about resiliency
2) Run a half-marathon in the fall

The exercise is quite straightforward, but the impact of mapping fear is extremely helpful. Dale Carnegie shared a cool perspective on this idea of inaction: "Inaction breeds doubt and fear. Action breeds confidence and courage. If you want to conquer fear, do not sit [at] home and think about it. Go out and get busy!"[11] Just think of how many things wouldn't have happened in your life if you hadn't taken that first step of action. So much of what we want is on the other side of fear. Try mapping this out to shine a light on what you are actually afraid of, and test that fear against the cost of inaction. Hopefully, this practice will help you put fear in its place, once and for all. And then when the fear pops back up, as it inevitably will, do the exercise again. Show fear just how rational you can be. Use your inner stoic to keep fear in perspective.

STEP 1

Writing a book about resiliency

DEFINE: What is the worst thing that could happen?	PREVENT: What can you do to prevent the worst thing from happening?	REPAIR: If the worst thing happens, how would you repair it?
1. No one reads it, and I am leaving an amazing, secure day job to be an author.	I can share it with people I know want to read it. My team can help identify groups who may want to read it. I can continue part time at the university for now.	I can host a focus group and learn how readers perceived my work. I could rerelease the book a year later with revisions. I can revisit the manuscript and adjust. I can go back to the academy somewhere.

Running a half-marathon

DEFINE	PREVENT	REPAIR
2. It hurts; it's hard.	I can actually follow a training plan and prioritize making time for getting my runs in (unlike past completed 21K runs when I showed up to races with little to no training). I can train in a manner that fosters body kindness.	Instead of just winging it, I can train for it properly and follow a training protocol. If need be, I can get a running coach or join a running club if I need more support. I can change the distance based on how my body responds, and accept it lovingly.

STEP 2

COST OF INACTION: What will it cost you if you don't do it?

Writing a book about resiliency

---

1. If I didn't share my work, I would regret it forever! I would be disappointed that I listened to the people in the stands (fear and strangers) instead of listening to other people in the arena. I would regret the greatest moments of heroism in my life being forgotten. There would be no record. I would let fear of judgement win at the cost of my voice and heart.

Running a half-marathon

---

2. I will spend another year randomly and sporadically running with no clear purpose, goal, or direction. I will hold the idea that long runs are for other people, not forty-one-year-old Robyne!

STEP 3

BENEFIT: What could go right?

Writing a book about resiliency

---

1. Someone could benefit from the words on these pages and I can help carry the load of life. I can have impact and help others see what they are capable of. People will say, "I can do hard things" to themselves and believe it. People will know my mom's name and what she meant to me. People will know they are already enough. I will have started a paradigm shift.

Running a half-marathon

---

2. Crossing that finish line! It will feel amazing to set a goal and achieve it. The post-race feeling of knowing I did it. The true pride of working toward health and wellness versus jean sizes and filters! Setting the example for my children. Being in my body and honouring what it is capable of.

"May your choices reflect your hopes, not your fears."

NELSON MANDELA

FEAR IN ACTION

Ava is our gymnast. What she can do with her body is truly remarkable. We celebrate that Ava is the toughest and strongest for her body-weight ratio in our family. Gymnastics is a sport of body and mind mastery. A gymnast's mind is as well trained as their shredded bodies. When Ava entered a new level of skills, she needed to strengthen those mental muscles in parallel with the intense physical requirements. Her body was strong and ready, but she told me that her anxiety was harder to train. I shared with Ava a classic breathing exercise known as "box breathing." Box breathing is when you control your breathing pattern in equal parts: Inhale for four seconds, hold for four seconds, exhale for four seconds, hold the empty space for four seconds. Repeat a few times. Imagine a box: breathe around all sides. You can even trace your finger in the shape of a box anywhere to help control your focus.

Ava also shared that she knew she was getting nervous when she felt butterflies in her stomach. After she could box breathe consistently, I invited her to take it to the next level with visualization to address those butterflies. When she became nervous at gymnastics, I encouraged her to imagine those butterflies in her stomach (nervous energy) and invite them to fly in a square in her mind. Imagine those butterflies in a huge open field, on a gorgeous and peaceful sunny afternoon, I told her. Feel the sun on your face and invite your butterflies to fly in harmony; invite them to fly in a perfect square.

Ava loved this exercise. I recall that at one competition I asked her how her butterflies were doing. She said that they were trying to fly in the square, but it was really windy there today!

After embracing this practice, Ava decided to name her butterflies. (A tip for remembering anything is to attach it to a memory you already have stored.) She gave her butterflies names from her own family. I love that she named them after some of her wise great-aunts: Kimberly, Barbara, Heather, Annamay. These butterflies represented the strong and mighty women who have more than 220 years of combined experience on this earth. Oh, how a child can soar when they are rooted in their family story.

Instead of becoming anxious when she got butterflies, Ava welcomed them as a gentle but fierce reminder of the women in her life who love her. She also named the field in which these butterflies play—Grammy's field, in honour of my mother and her grandmother.

Now, when Ava is challenged and feeling fear, this practice of "butterfly breathing" not only slows down her parasympathetic nervous system, it also showers her with knowledge of her rightful place within her family. Ava activates this experience whenever she needs it—whether at gymnastics, school, or even to help her wind down and find sleep at nighttime.

I remember sharing a similar box breathing technique when I was working with members of the military. During my talk, I left out the "naming butterflies" piece but did encourage the soldiers to control their breath through box breathing as a tactical strategy to slow down their minds and increase focus. I shared that Ava used this as an athlete prior to hurling herself through the air during tumbling lines. After my talk, a soldier came up to me and said that he too used this breathing technique. "Tell your daughter," he said, "that is exactly what I do when I am about to take my shot. I am a sniper and before I pull the trigger, that's what I do too, every time. We call it sniper breathing!" I am glad that this technique has been field-tested in battle, but I did not rush home and tell Ava. I smiled and let the soldier know we call it "butterfly breathing" and that Ava was eight.

EVERYDAY FEAR

Most of us don't sit too long with our fear every day. We know it is there, but thankfully the light of day and busyness help keep it buried. I remember that during very dark seasons of my life, nighttime brought relief from the everyday pressures, but brutal waves of intense fear also came at night. Seneca, the philosopher, explained that most people, as a coping strategy, spend most of their life in busyness. People are distracted by trivialities, noise, and pressures, not really being present or paying attention to anything at all. We certainly can spend an entire day without thinking about what truly matters or things of substance. Seneca said it becomes impossible to do any one thing well if one is busy with many things at once. The constant state of busyness lets fear silently build, and eventually this insurgence has us living a fear-laced life. How we think about fear can paralyze us. Using fear-setting helps: when you shower your fears with light and logic, they aren't as paralyzing. When we leave our fears unattended in our minds, that is where we get stuck and the damage happens. This is where we lose faith in our potential.

David Goggins is an author and retired Navy SEAL, considered by some to be the mentally toughest human on earth right now. In his book, *Can't Hurt Me: Master Your Mind and Defy the Odds*, Goggins recounts both physical and mental personal battles that seem to defy science. I read his book with my mouth open in shock the entire time. I remember thinking he must have different DNA and a different brain and body—no person could do what he's done! But at one point in his book he admits that he, too, feels fear. He shares that the greatest fear for him is getting to heaven and sitting with the book that shows him what his life could have been had he not given in to fear. Wow! Mind blown.

Imagine that each one of us has a book showing us what we are capable of experiencing, achieving, living, and being. Imagine that somehow our life's trajectory was mapped out to show us how we could have lived if only we had tried. When I read Goggins's idea, the first thing that came to mind was something Anaïs Nin said: "Life shrinks or expands in proportion to one's courage."[12] Then I thought about what my life book might say. In my mind, I bravely played around with these ideas: I had written my book; I was an author; I reclaimed my story; I found my voice; I helped people; I prevented one little girl from living a life defined by stigma; I helped one woman let go of the idea that she is her past; I boldly claimed that mistakes and events are just that, *not* characteristics; and people believed me.

I also thought about the potential rejection, harm, and negativity I could be opening myself and my family up to if my work wasn't well received. I landed on this idea: The cost of inaction is too great of a price to pay to protect my ego. My ego hasn't served me all that well in life, anyway. It was always my bruised, battered, and weary heart and mind that showed up every time I needed to keep going, despite all the hurt, pain, and fear. My ego always took off when life got tough. My ego yelled horribly mean things to me when I was spiralling out of control. My ego even honoured the people who were hurting me by agreeing with them and justifying why I deserved their mistreatment. Why would I give up on my dream of sharing this book with everyone for an ego that never stood by me? The ego worries about what the critics will say. The wounded but mighty heart of a resilient person knows they can handle whatever comes their way.

I hold this confidence because in my soul I know I am writing this book for the right reasons. I tell myself that a stranger I have yet to meet will be inspired by my story. She is waiting for this book right now. I will share knowledge, wisdom, or an idea she needs to hear, at the very moment she desperately needs to hear it. I am taking the fear and putting it in its rightful place—in a column on a fear-setting sheet, not standing in the way of my future. The benefits outweigh the costs of inaction. Here is where I make the choice and set an intention. I will be a lighthouse for others so they don't have to make the same mistakes I endured.

In that moment of wild and free thinking in my car, totally alone, reading Goggins's book, I decided to wholeheartedly commit to writing this book. I feel the fear. I see it. I know it is there. And I write these words anyway, for you and me both.

"

How different the world would be if our mistakes became lighthouses for people who are headed off-course instead of being a spotlight on our failures.

"

CHAPTER 5

STIGMA

STRESS AND FEAR create biological and emotional storms within, which get in the way of living a resilient life. These storms also make us feel that we are behind, not doing well enough, or are not good enough at managing our lives. We spend most of our time either regretting our past or worrying about the future. Stress and fear pull at us, holding us back. This seems like the ever-present dance or race of our existence. But there are also moments, often happening at the same time, that are positive and wonderful. In one area of our lives, we could be totally stressed out, and in another area, something special is unfolding. We constantly coexist with competing experiences.

I see it this way: Throughout our lives, as we grow and thrive, we will know joys and deep satisfaction that we are living well. We will also have setbacks, disappointments, hurt, and real pain. This is the truest take on life. As we navigate our life stories, all of us garner experiences, memories, and relationships, in a multitude of forms, and in the wins and the losses, if we choose to, we can see lessons. We learn. We change. We adapt. We become. Despite the fear and stressors, we persist.

However, often during these periods of difficulty, we encounter the third barrier that gets in the way of living a resilient life: stigma. Some are born into stigma, while others are thrown into it.

There are few things in this world that make me as frustrated as seeing people either living with stigma or being stigmatized; I even struggled with giving stigma its own chapter in this book because it bothers me so much! However, I decided to include and identify it as the third barrier because I believe it needs to be addressed, and I want to honour the people who share their stories with me. In these stories, I see stigma riddled throughout. I hear the labels. I feel the hurt. I know that pain. My heart recognizes the hurt in them. I believe that we must shine a light on what needs to be addressed. So here it is. Stigma, I am calling you out.

Stigma, by definition, is a mark of disgrace associated with a particular circumstance, quality, or person. I hope just hearing the definition creates a call to arms in your heart. A mark of disgrace! Are you kidding me? Why in this day and age are we still marking people! The word "stigma" comes from the Greek words referring to marking or tattooing. It was meant to signify an outward mark of criminals, slaves, or traitors, so that others could see that the person carrying the mark was blemished or "morally polluted." There is a long history across the globe of human branding as a means of control and punishment. Some were marked as belonging to a particular group. But more often, branding people was associated with someone who did not follow the rules. People were marked so everyone could see their shortcomings.

"Experience: that most brutal of teachers. But you learn, my God, do you learn."

C. S. LEWIS

I met a gentleman who survived the Holocaust as a young boy. On this man's weathered arm, I could still make out the tattoo forced upon him. He shared with me that this tattoo reminds him of the day he was separated from his mother. Through tired and cloudy eyes, he said, "That was a long time ago, dear. A very, very long time ago." This man has lived a marked life.

In 2000, researchers Steven Neuberg, Dylan Smith, and Terrilee Asher explained that people stigmatize as a means of improving their psychological welfare. It creates a clear divide. The team argued that stigmatizing is rooted in the need for people to work effectively and efficiently in groups. When someone violates the group norms, it threatens the welfare of the person who is following the norms, so they must mark out the person who doesn't fit or belong.[1] Stigma is meant to leave a mark.

Today stigma is not branded on our skin; it is branded on our souls. Stigma cannot coexist with compassion and empathy—it can occur only when someone is looking down on another. People have to mentally separate the person they are stigmatizing as different from them. Stigma is the ultimate tool of elitism. I have found that people who hold the tightest grip on stigma are often those who lack the basic understanding that we are more alike than we are different. These people lean into stereotypes and look past all the good just so they can prove to themselves that the stereotype they hold about the person they are stigmatizing is true. People who stigmatize tend to hold significant privilege and somehow believe they have earned it. The reality is that most people who hold such privilege were born into it and really didn't do anything to earn it themselves.

THE MANY FORMS OF STIGMA

Currently, there are multiple areas of stigmatization: race, mental health, physical health, family status, sexual orientation, socio-economic status, age, employment, even the type of food you eat or feed to your children. It is a sad state of affairs when so many people experience stigma, ranging in severity, every single day of their lives—in person and online. Stigma comes in many forms and attacks from all sides. People are left living within the blast radius of a force that hits from outside and within. No matter what you call it or the target, stigma is a form of dehumanization and discrimination.

Patrick W. Corrigan and John R. O'Shaughnessy have identified three types of stigma.[2]

1 **Structural stigma** is when there are policies or practices within private and public institutions that restrict opportunities or disallow participation—for example, not hiring someone with a criminal record or reducing parental rights for those with a history of mental illness.

2 **Social stigma** is when people within a society hold a bias, avoidance, discomfort, or overt discrimination against a person who is somehow distinguished from the norm. For example, in health care, research shows that patients with lung cancer receive poorer treatment (even if they are non-smokers) than other cancer patients, since people hold the belief that their cancer was preventable. Another example is people being stigmatized based on the amount of space their bodies occupy in the world. Our bodies are too fat or too thin, never just right.

3 **Self stigma** is when a person internalizes all the messaging about what the norm is, believes the stereotypes, sees how they don't belong, and then lives with deep shame and social rejection. For example, a single parent is told by society that she failed; the system tells her she can't qualify for a mortgage since she is the sole provider; and she feels deep shame and guilt when she fills out the children's school forms as a "Non-intact family." (I can't let that example go without a comment—WTF! I happen to know plenty of "intact" families that are off the rails. My heart screams when I hear parents say they are staying in dysfunctional and damaging relationships "for the kids." You don't stay for the kids, you leave for the kids, if it is unhealthy and dysfunctional. Please don't stay and teach them a lifetime of bad relationship behaviours.)

A fourth type of stigma is emerging, called association stigma (also known as courtesy stigma). This is when a person is stigmatized for being linked to someone else who is stigmatized. An example of association stigma is how parents of a child with an addiction are treated by others, or a health care worker who works at a needle exchange program being judged for who she helps. They are viewed as culpable or enabling the undesired trait or behaviour.

THE EFFECTS OF STIGMA

It is not often that researchers agree, but when it comes to the effects of stigma, they are quite unanimous. Stigma hurts. Stigma is damaging. Stigma ruins lives. Stigma harms potential. Stigma prevents people from seeking help.

People who are stigmatized are more likely to experience all sorts of mental health challenges, including depression, isolation, negative self-esteem, and even suicidal ideation. In their study, Patrick W. Corrigan and Deepa Rao explained that the diminished self-esteem that accompanies stigma robs people of social opportunities.[3] The mental health literature demonstrates that the stigma associated with mental health conditions prevents people from accessing services and getting help. I have held a distraught parent who said it would have been easier to hear that their teenager had cancer than schizophrenia. This is just so sad and wrong on so many levels. Fear and misunderstanding lead to prejudice, discrimination, and hate. It is because of stigma that people are scared to ask for help, that they and their families suffer.

Stigma Creates Shame

Each one of the four types of stigma previously mentioned creates the same by-product: shame. Stigma is the outside world holding a belief about us; shame is how we internalize that belief. When we explore shame, the conversation often includes guilt. I think it is helpful to draw the distinction here: shame and guilt are not the same thing. Guilt is the feeling that you did something wrong. Shame is the feeling that you are wrong. Guilt means we broke a rule, an expectation, or standard. Shame is the belief that we are broken. Shame screams we are flawed, irrepairable, and ultimately unlovable. Shame keeps us in the shadows. Shame sounds like, "If people knew the real me, they would be disgusted"; "If people knew the real me, they would leave"; "If people knew the real me, I would be alone forever."

I cannot say another word about shame without mentioning the amazing Brené Brown. Brown is the ultimate shame researcher and storyteller. She describes shame as the unspoken epidemic in our society. As she writes in *The Gifts of Imperfection*, "Shame is the intensely painful feeling or experience of believing we are flawed and therefore unworthy of acceptance and belonging. Women often experience shame when they are entangled in a web of layered, conflicting and competing social-community expectations. Shame creates feelings of fear, blame and disconnect." [4]

Shame is a visceral feeling that can strike at any moment and can have a long history in our personal narrative. There are layers upon layers that are both internal and external. The world teaches us from an early age what is expected of us. When there is any deviation from the norm, we learn shame. We carry it with us in all that we do, both consciously and unconsciously. It is like the monster-under-the-bed feeling: part of us knows it is not real, but we are still afraid to pull a leg out from under the covers, just in case!

Shaming others has become a common form of relational aggression. It is one of the most common socially acceptable weapons used in society today. Sometimes it is delivered in jest, passively, with little to no regard for the impact, although it can also be weaponized with full intention of maximum damage. People can be shamed for anything: being too thin, too fat, too tall, too short, too healthy, too unhealthy, too committed, too lazy, too troubled, too boring, too social, too isolated, too motivated, too passive, too slow, too fast, too smart, too rich, too poor, or simply because they have freckles and red hair. I lived this one every day, starting in kindergarten. Absolutely everything and anything about us can be judged by others and can lead to shaming—it can be as random as the type of dog you own! Here is just one example I recently experienced that I did not see coming.

Part of navigating my big life is my ritual of "winning my mornings." Winning your mornings is when you protect the first hour of your day. You do all the things that you need to do to set yourself up for a positive day. For me, it starts with waking up by my alarm clock every morning at the exact same time. First test of the day—Robyne versus the world—do not hit snooze. If you pass this first test, you are already winning the morning. Test two is making my bed. Yes, even in hotel rooms, that bed is made. You get the idea. Simple and actionable items that create a pattern of routine.

I feed the animals, drink water, spend time in reflection and prayer, drink coffee, and make time for movement. Movement is for joy, renewal, and pleasure. Movement is never for fitness' sake. I move to build my power, resiliency, and endurance.

So, in essence, winning your morning means you purposely set out to do things that support you feeling like your best self early in your day. The best way to *not* win your morning is to check your email. You do not want to start your day by being reactive to the world. Your inbox is a collection of everyone else's agenda for your day. It is not your agenda. You will get to that inbox eventually, but not in the first hour—that hour is yours. Sure, you might spend it with kids and others, but you oversee the energy and focus you bring to that hour. Protect it.

So, part of my being-in-motion practice in the mornings is to walk our dogs before anyone else is awake. I love to experience the world while she is in stillness and peace. It did not take many early morning walks for Luna and Apollo, our pups, to start holding me accountable to this ritual. Clearly, they like to win their mornings as well.

One morning, I was approached by a stranger on the trail while walking. Yes, I was surprised seeing another human out that early on purpose too. The woman stopped to ask me about my dogs. She was curious about their breeds. I explained that Apollo was a little bit of this and that, a black lab and border collie cross, and Luna was a chocolate lab. The woman recoiled from us in disgust. She then proceeded to tell me that it was because of people like me that there are thousands of dogs dying in shelters while people boutique-shop purebred dogs. She blamed me for the pet over-population problem in our country.

Well, six in the morning is a little early for social shaming. I did not think too long or hard before responding. I wish I could share with you that I had some brilliant comeback that taught that woman a valuable life lesson, but I cannot. In that moment, all that came to me was this: "If you want to shame me, I am a working mother who feeds our children Kraft Dinner a lot, and it isn't even organic, and those same kids have been known to take Lunchables to school in a pinch! I am a parent and a professional. I live with real shame of dropping the ball somehow, every single day!"

Apparently, that is what my big lie or secret confession was. In that moment, it felt like, finally, the right time to let my truth shine. If this woman was going to shame me, she might as well shame me about something I feel shame about. And yes, dear reader, despite all the work I do, I still feel the deep shame of feeding our children Kraft Dinner from time to time. How ridiculous is that?

Society has worked extremely hard to build these narratives of what is right and wrong. And we have been taking them in since toddlerhood. So, the better question is: How do we disarm shame? Thankfully, Brené Brown has the solution: authenticity. If we own our reality, they can never use it against us in the same way again. I came upon and truly embraced this idea the day I released my Unsinkable story into the world. I recommitted to authenticity. Sharing my Unsinkable story was the line in the sand—I finally called out shame. The same day the story dropped, I posted a message on Instagram that read: "When you own your own story, no one can use it against you." I sent that out into the world like a weary battle cry against shame. I will not let you or anyone else hold against me my mistakes, setbacks, mental health challenges, or anything else you do not think is good enough about me. My story is mine. My life is mine.

And you know what? Something amazing happens when you look shame in the eye and say, *no more*. When you pull yourself out of the shadows and reclaim all of your life, shame loses power over you. You regain your footing. You stand in your truth. Battered and bruised, messy and irreparable, not perfect but present, you fall in love with your imperfect self and become your own protector and warrior. You stop fighting yourself and start fighting *for* yourself. You become the person you needed all your life. The one that sees your vulnerability and accepts you completely as you are.

So, yes, I have made major life mistakes. I have hurt people. I have been hurt. I could have done life differently, but I did not. My story has light and dark. There is good and bad. But it is all mine. It is striking that as soon as you accept yourself as you are, the people who do not like you become so irrelevant. Here is a gentle saying I like to repeat to keep this in focus: "On the outside, authentically humble; on the inside, warrior confident." My family motto is *Virescit Vulnere Virtus*: Courage grows strong at a wound. My wounds are the origins of my courage. My wounds prove that I can do hard things.

We need to be able to let go of stigma. What are you carrying subconsciously that is holding you back or keeping you stuck? Those parts inevitably bleed into the rest of our lives if left unobserved or unattended, and hinder the things that actually matter. I think this happens for us more than we realize. Practicing resiliency starts with being honest with ourselves and looking inward. This is not only hard work; it is heart work. No one can do this for you. Ultimately it is up to you.

Disarming Shame with Authenticity

Here is Brené Brown's manifesto against shame. Let us join our voices and be imperfect here together. Remember, how we combat shame is through authenticity.

AUTHENTICITY is a daily practice.

Choosing authenticity means: cultivating the COURAGE to be emotionally honest, to set boundaries, and to allow ourselves to be vulnerable; exercising the COMPASSION that comes from knowing that we are all made of strength and struggle and connected to each other through a loving and resilient human spirit; nurturing the CONNECTION and sense of belonging that can only happen when we let go of what we are supposed to be and embrace who we are.

Authenticity demands WHOLEHEARTED living and loving—even when it's hard, even when we're wrestling with the shame and fear of not being good enough, and especially when the joy is so intense that we're afraid to let ourselves feel it.

Mindfully practicing authenticity during our most SOUL-SEARCHING struggles is how we invite GRACE, JOY, and GRATITUDE into our lives.[5]

We must stand up and walk out of our history. As I've said, there is no future in our past. We are never too old, and it is never too late to change our course.

THE BIG IDEAS OF PART II

In Part II, I introduced the common variables—stress, fear, and stigma—that impede a person's capacity for resiliency, and offered some practices so you can start doing the heavy heart work it takes to become more resilient.

In my practitioner field, we talk about the idea of holding space—the art of being with someone without judgement. It is the practice of showing empathy and accepting someone's truth and reality without jumping in with solutions or commentary. Holding space is a transformational approach to being there for someone else. We are willing to walk alongside another person on their journey without making it about us.

I am often asked how I can work with people in such difficult times and seasons of their lives. My practice of educating, counselling, coaching, and leading has spanned two decades. That work has brought me into so many situations, environments, and experiences I never imagined, and I have worked with people from so many backgrounds, that I needed to spend time reflecting on that question and its answer. What I came upon was that I am okay sitting in discomfort. I am comfortable in the uncomfortable. I have sat in hospitals, principals' offices, police departments, prisons, Olympic sporting venues, addiction centres, funeral homes, and even morgues. I have witnessed the common humanity and shared experience of pain. When you learn how to be okay in the discomfort, stress, and fear, the power that you give those heavy emotions can be reclaimed. You learn how to hold space for

"Learn to adjust yourself
to the conditions you have
to endure, but make a point of
trying to alter or correct
conditions so that they are
most favorable to you."

WILLIAM FREDERICK BOOK

the negative parts of life and trust in your capacity to endure. As the old saying goes, "Calm seas do not produce skilled sailors." We learn more about ourselves in the storms. My goal is to hold that deep sense of calm in the form of trust and conviction that all will be well in any storm.

Every time we can sit in discomfort and not run from it, we strengthen both our capacity to do hard things and our belief that we can. We retrain our brains to understand that although the situation is unpleasant, we are okay. Our survival rate, on any day we are alive, is 100 per cent!

I recall sitting with a woman who had just lost her husband. He had died that morning and she held a vigil, sitting in a chair right next to the bed, as his body remained untouched. The nurses instructed her to say goodbye and call them when she was ready to have the body removed. The immediate family had said their goodbyes and left. I happened to be the last person in the room with the woman and her husband's body. I asked her if she wanted me to stay or leave, and she invited me to sit next to her. I stayed for over three hours. A few words were shared, stories recounted, but mostly it was silent. The nurses let us be. No one interrupted us. In her own time, the woman released her husband's hand, looked at me, and said, "Thank you. I wasn't sure I was going to remember how to breathe without him."

Life is going to continue. Despite the stress, fear, and stigma, we can persist. We can keep breathing.

My intention in Part II was to prepare you the best I can for what the obstacles look like. Next, let me show you how we can build our capacity for resiliency. Everyone has the capacity to form and hold a baseline of resiliency. I'll introduce you to my model of resiliency based on the five core traits: belonging, perspective, acceptance, hope, and humour. These factors make resiliency possible.

PART III

THE FIVE PILLARS

THE BASELINE FOR RESILIENCY

66

I was so desperate to feel as though I belonged in my own life.

99

CHAPTER 6

BELONGING

OUR DEEPEST DESIRE is to belong—to be truly seen and to matter. We long to achieve empathic attunement even if only for a short time. Empathic attunement is that moment when someone looks at you as if you are the only person in the world. You are completely accepted and truly understood by that person. You know they have your back. We need to matter to someone so deeply that it penetrates our very soul.

Belonging is often glossed over in the discussions about resiliency since the emphasis seems to be on toughening up or going against the norm or being a lone wolf. Going at life alone is not the answer. The answer is finding our place in the world and being seen for who we are. This is where we find our deepest strength. Brené Brown explained that it is "those who have a strong sense of connection and belonging that have the courage to be imperfect."[1] Here lies the first pillar of resiliency: belonging.

"A single twig breaks, but the bundle of twigs is strong."

TECUMSEH

Dan Buettner, the founder of the Blue Zones research initiative, discovered what he explained were the five zones in the world where people lived the longest and healthiest lives. In 2005, the Blue Zone research program identified values associated with human longevity. These researchers studied populations of people who were most likely to live to be centenarians (one hundred and over). Among the nine common dominators, belonging was key.[2] Our greatest chance of surviving and thriving is when we are accepted into a community, and we wholeheartedly believe we are part of the very fabric of what makes that community. For some of us, that community could be our family system. For others, it may be a self-generated tribe of friends or a professional identity that forms an emotional safe zone. The idea is that together we are stronger and alone we flounder.

The military, with all its customs, traditions, and rituals, is a prime example. I have spoken with soldiers who after serving a tour of duty struggle with the lack of connection they feel with their loved ones once they are back home. They share that they just do not feel as close to their wives, husbands, or partners as they do to their platoon mates. They have experienced empathic attunement so deeply, in such a stressful state, that other relationships seem lacking somehow. I also see this with new parents, whereby a person may feel disconnected from their partner once the baby is born. The person may feel as though they have never been looked at the way the mom is looking at her new baby. Mom's eyes are filled with such devotion, loyalty, protection, and care for that new baby. Empathic attunement is a special shared experience and a powerful bond.

Evolutionary psychology has summarized the need to belong and the bonding to another person as the core of our human survival. When a new mother breastfeeds her baby, the distance from the crook of her arm that cradles the baby's head to her eyes is the exact visual distance a baby can see. Hence, when mom is feeding her baby, all the baby can see is her face, which creates a bond. Baby smiles, mom smiles: the baby has a protector. Evolution didn't take any chances. Just to seal the deal, as mom breastfeeds, oxytocin is released in her bloodstream. She is being flooded with the bonding hormone. Evolution and biology unite to pave a connection that transcends life itself. A mother is always a mother, even after her children have grown. And when mother and child are separated, the phenomena known as *Mizpah* (the Hebrew word for connection, the emotional bond between two people apart) occurs.

Psychologists John Bowlby and Mary Ainsworth studied the connection between a child and their parent and coined the term "attachment theory." Attachment theory can be summarized by Bowlby's famous phrase, "from the cradle to the grave." This suggests that the attachment style we embody in infancy carries us from our earliest days to our death.[3] Relationships with others are crucial for our physical, social, and moral development. Researchers have devoted their lives to explaining how our different attachment styles impact us across our lifespan.[4]

THE STORIES WE CARRY

Once we have established trust and a bond to secure our survival, we can start exploring the big world around us. As we grow and age, we start building wider social nets. With exposure to those nets, we learn to take on roles that help inform our identity. Ideally, the roles we play, which become our identity, serve us well, but this is not always the case. Even before toddlerhood, we start developing an internal script that tells us a story of who we are and where we fit in. As school-aged children, we decide on a label, perhaps of our own choosing but often from someone else. This label could be: I am a good student. During this time, it is in a relatively conscious state that we reflect on that label and decide if it fits. Regardless of whether it is positive or negative, eventually that label moves from the conscious into the subconscious, resulting in the embodied belief that it defines who we are.

Now, let us unpack this even more. Let us say the label I carry is that I am not a math person. I then seek out events and evidence to support this label. Our personal views direct our behaviour. I find it fascinating that "I'm not a math person" or "I can't do math" is so widely accepted in our culture. Few people would disclose or say out loud that they cannot read! Yet "not a math person" is a means of forming solidarity with others who hold a similar belief about themselves.

As we navigate this world, we become a constellation of stories that form our identities, and these identities help shape how we continue to find communities in which we can belong.

Take a moment to think about all the roles and communities you belong to. I am a mother, a daughter, a wife, an educator, a scholar, a redhead, a descendant from Scotland, a coach, a teammate, an emerging author—the list could go on almost endlessly. Holding multiple and sweeping roles helps protect us and these roles serve as avenues to belonging. When any of our roles end, we grieve. This is evidence that these roles are so vitally important to us.

I remember sitting across a table from a national-level basketball player who had recently left professional sports. This man, standing six foot nine, had tears rolling down his cheeks as he shared with me that all he had ever known was how to be a basketball player. With a raspy voice, he said, "I wasn't done playing basketball, but basketball was done with me." It is not uncommon to see people crumble when their roles end. Absolutely every life change is double-sided. We celebrate parenthood but are mindful that our world as we know it will never be the same. We are exhausted driving our children all over the country to participate in sports, rehearsals, playdates, and competitions, but the moment we drop them off at school, we are gutted.

Our roles make up who we are and how the world sees us. Our roles help us forge belonging. Now, what happens when we feel we do not belong anywhere? What if we never established that connection early in life that serves as our compass to find more connection and community?

SOCIAL PAIN AND THE NEED TO BELONG

In the early 2000s, I completed an internship as part of my behavioural science training at the maximum-security prison in Kingston, Ontario. Kingston Penitentiary was the oldest prison in Canada (opened in 1835 and closed in 2013). Forged out of limestone, this building, with over a hundred years of stories, holds a commanding presence along the shores of the Saint Lawrence River. Marred by a long history of imprisoning children, women, and men during the formation of Canada as a country, this thunderous building is etched into my mind. I was eerily aware of each minute I spent working inside those walls. As days, weeks, and months past, I never lost the feeling that I was walking upon land that had held broken people and those who had broken others. Kingston Pen is now a museum, open to the public with guided tours operated by Corrections Canada. You can see the very walls that housed Canada's most notorious criminals, including Grace Marks, who committed her alleged crimes in 1843. (Margaret Atwood's 1996 novel *Alias Grace* is based on her story.) She was pardoned in 1872.

One typical day, while I was working within the treatment facility, there was a lockdown at another part of the institution. Regular programming was postponed. One of the psychologists asked me if I wanted to go onto the floor to play cards. We spent the afternoon playing cards with some of the inmates. That afternoon was one of the most prolific learning experiences of my life. I learned the raw and unabridged version of social justice, violence, racism, prejudice, classism, and deviant behaviour from people who had been marked by society.

One story stood out to me. The man shared that he had been incarcerated for longer than he had ever lived on the outside. I could not begin to wrap my head around this fact. Apparently, when he was a young adult, he had been recruited by a gang. He explained that, finally, after years of being bounced around, not fitting in anywhere, and not really having a family, he had found his people. The gang became his family. To be guaranteed membership in his new family and solidify his place, he had to commit a heinous crime. He shared that he is part of a family now both inside and outside of the prison walls. He said that they would help him build a new life once he was released. He mattered to them and they mattered to him.

We will go to great lengths, even sacrificing our freedom, to belong to something or a group of people. Michael Carlie writes on this topic.[5] The draw to a gang is a means of replacing a nonexistent or damaged family system. Naomi Eisenberger and Matthew Lieberman's work can also help understand the social pain that comes from rejection, loss, separation, and breakups.[6] They write that social pain is felt as deeply as physical pain and postulate that we need connection as much as we need security, food, and shelter. Humans will go to extreme lengths to find somewhere to belong.

At no other point in history have we been so connected yet so isolated and lonely. Connection has become competitive. How many likes, followers, and retweets one can get have become markers of popularity. Before, it used to be how many people you sat with at lunch in the cafeteria, but now it is how viral you can go!

People are hurting. We feel alone. We feel like fakes and frauds. Imposter syndrome is not just for professionals anymore. When I think about the abundance of opportunities for connection but the reality of loneliness, it reminds me of a line from the lyrical ballad *The Rime of the Ancient Mariner*: "Water, water every where / nor any drop to drink."[7] We are thirsting for true connection and meaning in our relationships, but we are filled with feelings of lack and inauthenticity.

Now, let us dive into possible solutions for this problem. To start, please hear: you are not alone. Many of us think comparative social media, hyper-competitiveness with our peers, and trying to fit in is a waste of time and energy. It is actually plain gross and self-destructive. Social media is a highlight reel that people want you to see, and what we see is skewing our perspective and contributing to us feeling bad about ourselves. What is portrayed in media is not sustainable or satisfying. It is helpful to instead seek out the social media platforms that are pushing back against this trend—they are out there! (A shout-out to the many Canadian nutritionists who are doing this good work.) We will talk more about how to change our habits later, but in the meantime, it is important to recognize that it is okay if we intellectually know social comparison is harmful but do it anyway.

FINDING CONNECTION

Making new friends is relatively straightforward for many children. They are in a shared environment, like a playground. One child asks another child their name. Maybe how they are, or if they like dogs. And then, ta-dah: they are instant friends.

As adults, making friends and connections is hard. I see the evidence for this often with sports families. I have witnessed and worked with adults who cry when their child is released or cut from a sports team. The parents are devastated on one level for their child but mainly because the other parents of the team are their friend circle. In parenthood, our sense of community usually comes from our children's worlds. For others, it could be when they leave their job: they lose their work family or their social life. So, where do we go to find connection outside of these social networks?

To start, I think it is important to foster connection with yourself first. Connecting and belonging in adulthood needs to start with your relationship with yourself, then your relationships with others, followed by your relationships with the broader world.

Who Are You and Who Are You Becoming?

In the classic romantic comedy *Runaway Bride*, starring Julia Roberts as Maggie Carpenter, after a series of failed relationships, Maggie is left lost. She does not even know how she likes her eggs cooked! Her likes and preferences have been influenced by her relationships. A dear friend takes the time to prepare Maggie every variety of eggs so she can relearn her preferences. Thankfully, at any point in our lives we can relearn and reconnect with who we are.

I invite you take a moment and ask yourself if you even truly like the things you think you like. Let us start with a few questions for reflections. You can pick and choose which ones you like. There is no right or wrong answer. I invite you to notice if you do not like a question, and maybe spend some time there. It is helpful to notice when our natural resistance meter is engaged, as doing so can help gauge what is really going on under the surface. Usually it is a sign we touched a nerve, which is always helpful for self-discovery.

Just a few gentle questions to start the reflection process:

- Do I like me?
- Do I think I am a likeable person?
- Do I like spending time with me?
- What makes me feel competent?
- What makes me feel strong?
- What feelings do I not like feeling?
- What feelings do I want to feel more?
- What is my personal goal and mission statement for this year?
- If I stay on this life course, will I end up where I want to be at the end?
- Where do I find my joy? Peace? Calm?
- When will I finally forgive myself for my mistakes?
- How can I strengthen my sense of purpose?
- How can I strengthen my sense of worth?

- What is my "why"? Why am I here?
- Who do I want to be? What roles, identities, and traits truly fit with the person I am and want to become?
- Reflect on a time you felt proud of yourself. How can you have more moments like that?

Again, these are just a few questions to prompt your thinking about getting to know yourself and to identify your personal values and goals. If this is too much coming at you, you can spend some time on lighter questions! How do you like your eggs? That matters too.

Now you can reflect on your family or social supports:

- What is working?
- What is not working?
- Who is in your corner?
- Who has your back?
- Where are you safe?
- Where are you truly seen?
- Where are you the most like the "you" you want to be?

A wonderful lesson I came upon is that not every person has to fulfil every part of our safety network. Learning how to discern where to go for certain supports and encouragement is vital to building depth and breadth in our safe places and connections. However, I see people who try to create extremely large teams of support. This is not necessary. From my work I believe we need only one "caring companion champion" to help hold us up. I think of this person as someone who will stand in front of us to protect us if needed. They will stand beside us in respect. They will stand behind us as the encourager. And they will defend us, even from ourselves, if called upon.

"Alone we can do so little; together we can do so much."

HELEN KELLER

In professional boxing, the athlete gets to bring two people to the ring with them: the cornerman and the cutman. Throughout the course of the fight, these two stand vigilant but at a distance. Only during the breaks between rounds can either of them enter the ring to coach and administer to their fighter and repair any damage the fighter has taken on. As a boxer's career ebbs and flows, they may change who is in their corner for the fight.

People come and go. Roles people hold in our lives sometimes change—by choice or otherwise—or they remain a constant. That is part of evolution and progression. If your ring team grows with you, maybe you keep the same team for your whole life. Other times, change happens, and we let people go or they leave us. We grieve. Then we bring a new team on board. But the key idea to remember is that no boxer ever goes into a fight without a team in their corner. We can learn a great lesson from the best sports movie franchise of all time, Rocky. Even when one of our cornermen leaves us, they are still in every corner of our heart and soul. We all need a Mickey to our Rocky—someone who loves us unconditionally, sees all of us, but will also tell us what we need to hear, not just what we want to hear. As Mickey yelled at Rocky in Rocky's darkest hour, "Get up, you son of a bitch! Mickey loves you."

Community Connections

Once you get a sense of you and who you really want to become, and how you want to be seen, it is time to think about your relationships and connections in the real world. This takes bravery and commitment. Making connections is not for the faint of heart. As Eisenberger and Lieberman's work explains, rejection can lead to social pain.[8] But it can also lead to community and joy, which can help foster your resilient self. It is okay to walk gently in the direction you wish to travel. So now, let us take a moment to reflect on community.

- What communities are you already a part of?
- Which ones serve you well?
- Which communities do you choose versus join out of obligation?
- What kind of community do you want to be a part of?

It is amazing to see just how many real-life clubs, groups, organizations, and communities you can join. Remember, there is a difference between fitting in and belonging. It is normal at the beginning to feel like you don't belong, but over time, as you strengthen your commitment to being part of that community, the sense of belonging will increase. What is important is to first identify the value or group identity that best fits with your goal. For example, if you want to be healthier, maybe you think about joining a gym. This seems logical. Unfortunately, many people set out to join something that is too unfamiliar as a starting point. We need to build community gradually.

Say someone decides to join a gym and immediately signs up for a die-hard CrossFit program. I see this sort of thing often. People want to take part in a new community, so they go to the centre of all the action. This isn't ideal—it creates friction because as soon as they walk in, they start comparing themselves, and then quickly decide that they do not belong there. Or they stick through the brutal workout, driven by pride, and then they can barely walk the next day! They reflect that eating Oreos and watching Netflix (their previous behaviour) never made them incapable of walking up a flight of stairs, so they therefore conclude they just do not belong to this type of class.

Or another example: say you decide to go vegan for both ethical and cosmetic reasons. You feel like garbage as your body adjusts to a new food system, so you decide, "This isn't for me." You go all-in quickly and then regret it just as quickly. Another example is how some people come out. They feel like they need to rush right into the hallmarks of the queer community—for example, by going to a gay bar. But they might not be comfortable there yet. And members of that community might shame them for not being "queer enough" because they're bi, or asexual, or were formally in a hetero relationship, or don't wear the right clothes.

I invite you to be gentle with your steps as you walk toward forming new communities. Little steps in the right direction are important. Let us say you want to be more active. Is there a type of class for beginners you could try? I suggest starting with an activity that is rooted in self-compassion as a good starting point. Perhaps gentle yoga. I think starting with gentle yoga is a better choice than going out to an advanced hot yoga class with goats and Lululemon models! Start small; build connections with purpose and intention. Strive to find something that fits you, not just something you can fit in with.

Starting small with intention is more sustainable in the long run. In society right now there is an outside pressure that is yelling at us to "jump in, just f*ck it, do it!" This pressure reminds me of traditional peer pressure in high school: "Oh, c'mon... everyone is doing it... why are you so scared? You're so lame." Being tentative, cautious, and purposeful is not being scared, a chicken, or boring. It is smart!

I find it fascinating that after all this time, with all the workout programs I have done, walking is the only exercise I have stuck with for thirty years. My HIIT workout was ninety days compared with walking at 10,950 days so far. Small changes have huge gains when they are practiced consistently, purposefully, and with intention. I remind myself every day that we can never hate ourselves healthy. We cannot use movement as food correction. We cannot shame ourselves into healing. Wellness is not all or nothing. It is micro-behaviours that we do each day that are positive, restorative, and kind. We do not have to wait for a Monday to start practicing wellness. We do not have to have that "last supper" before we start eating for nourishment. (I call it the last supper because before starting the next new diet fad, people often have that last supper of food they're not "supposed" to have. This is not wellness.)

FAITH

At the beginning of this chapter, I shared with you the work of the Blue Zones research team. Another common denominator of health and longevity that intersects with belonging is a person's faith. This is an example of how we connect to the world around us. Faith is extremely personal and cultural, but there are many similar characteristics between world faiths. Belonging to something that is greater than yourself matters. Faith communities create places of belonging by sharing a collective consciousness of trusting in something that we cannot see, count, or measure. With all religions and faiths, there is the idea that you can believe in something that exists outside of time, remains constant, and is ever-unchanging. The unchangeability is something that people can connect to and depend on. Faith, religion, or spirituality can act as

"I already knew
what you meant. I did not
need a lifetime of
missing you to show me."

JMSTORM

a stable resting place for us when we're weary. When life is complicated, unforgiving, and relentless, as it often can be, having a rock upon which you can rest and cast your worries is the universal root of belonging and being connected to something greater. Our faith also has the capacity to bind us to our past, ground us in our future, and foster hope for tomorrow.

I recently talked with a mother who lost her adult son to suicide. She shared with me that she now "belongs" to a group she never wanted to be part of—those who have buried a child. In her deepest sorrow she also found an unexpected sense of belonging within her faith. She shared that she trusted her son was finally at peace after years of torment. Another mother I talked with told me that she had recently lost her infant. She didn't have forty years of memories to hold on to, like the other mother. This young mom shared with me that she actually sought out religion after she lost her baby. She envied the peace her husband could find through prayer. This mother wanted to believe in something that said she would see her daughter again. With newfound faith, she too found comfort not of this earth.

Everyone's experience is unique. I am disheartened when people feel embarrassed or ashamed to share with me that their sense of belonging comes from their faith. This is not something anyone should be ashamed of. Our faith is no less valid than someone's inspiration, motivation, and drive through nature, art, or music. I invite you to celebrate wherever you can find community, strength, purpose, and peace of mind. You do you. Don't worry so much where you find renewal and rest. Being able to be faith-filled is a gift many people strive to experience, yet it remains elusive to so many.

Knowing who we are, where we belong, and to whom we are bonded is vital for everyday resiliency. Our inner strength can be summoned by tapping into our true self and the memories and experiences of our relationships with our loved ones, present and past. I believe that all the people in our lives with whom we have shared empathic attunement are always with us. We can lean into our memories and create a sense of safety wherever we are.

I also believe that the relationship you have with yourself, and how you treat yourself, will directly impact how you let others treat you. Know your worth! Honour your communities and tend to them carefully and with purpose. However, be mindful: if you spend a great deal of time around anyone, you will eventually become like them. If you do not want to be like them, don't hang around them. Researchers have concluded that we become like the five people we spend most of our time with.[9] Choose carefully. And remember: you are one of the five!

66

Our perspective is a constellation of attitudes, mindsets, and emotions that form a lens through which we see the world.

99

CHAPTER 7

PERSPECTIVE

DEFINING PERSPECTIVE IN art is relatively straightforward. It is how a two-dimensional object can be represented, for instance through drawing, to give the right impression of height, width, depth, and position, when we look at it from a certain point of view. Perspective-taking in our own lives is not as clear. Our perspective is a constellation of attitudes, mindsets, and emotions that form a lens through which we see the world. Knowing the origins of how we developed our perspective and even the notion of changing our perspectives could very well become our life's work. This concept of personal perspective-taking is the second pillar in the resiliency model.

Perspective can be viewed as an alignment between two key parts: attitudes or mindset, and emotions. Let us look at attitude or mindset first. Carol Dweck brought the term "mindset," specifically "growth mindset" and "fixed mindset," into popularity with her book *Mindset: The New Psychology of*

Success. This book has significantly impacted education for good reason. Dweck proposed how we can frame challenges to be more useful and helpful for our development. Mindset is the attitude we take when we meet a challenge. It can also be seen by how we interpret causality to an event.

For example, my son Hunter is an exceptionally skilled basketball player. People say he is a natural athlete. Other people say he is hard-working and disciplined. The first idea—Hunter is a natural—suggests he is a capable athlete because of predetermined factors such as his height, weight, and IQ. These traits are relatively fixed. Conversely, the person who recognizes Hunter's accomplishments as resulting from dedication, hard work, and sacrifice is showing their growth mindset. They attribute his success and developed skills to his commitment to training more than twenty hours a week on the court.

Of course, everyone has a baseline for relative ability (the fixed traits), but what we *do* with that baseline is more indicative of what we are truly capable of becoming. Recognizing and believing that effort, persistence, commitment, and dedication contribute to overall success in sport or in life is the heart of a growth mindset.

The attitude we bring to our learning and challenges is extremely important. A positive attitude can even fill the gap when there is a lack of skill: the mindset literature suggests that if we present feedback to someone in a manner that captures their potential of acquiring the lacking skill, it will motivate them to continue—for example, "You don't quite have that correct, yet." The operative word is "yet." When we hear that, it sends us the message that we could someday have the skill. In contrast, when we hear "you can't do that," period, it suggests we never will be able to. Although the mindset literature holds true here, I think what can be added to this idea is the importance of the person truly believing that the "yet," the potential, is within their ability. If a teacher tells their student that they don't understand a math concept like BEDMAS (PEMDAS for you American readers) *yet*, with the hope that the student will feel encouraged, but the student doesn't believe that they will ever understand algebra, then all the good intentions and positive talk fall on barren soil. Hope and optimism aren't implanted in the student's heart, just more disappointment and feeling like they aren't ever going to get it.

To address this additional dimension of mindset and the potential of it not working if a person doesn't believe a task possible, let's look at the role of emotion. Although behavioural scientists have argued and demonstrated that cognition (thinking) comes first, then emotion or affect, for many of us the feelings seem directly linked or concurrent. The time between the thought and feeling is so close together that it seems as if they are happening at the same time. In my definition of perspective as it relates to resiliency, I view mindset and emotion as allies, not as cause-and-effect variables. Positive thinking is awfully popular in the self-help realm right now; however, again, I wonder how many people think they are doing it wrong because they don't *feel* that messaging. Getting our feelings in alignment matters too.

I have long attested that the greatest distance in the world sometimes is the delta between your head and your heart. Intellectually I can believe or know something thoroughly. I can know it is true with all of my intellectual might, but my heart may still feel anxious, scared, or achy. Or my mind races back to a thought over and over despite "knowing better."

For me, perspective must go beyond the intellectual practice of positivity and potential. We must align our head and heart. Through this alignment we can truly know and believe and therefore act accordingly. We need to know and feel we are tapping into authenticity. Again, it is our mindset and attitude, cascading through our feelings and tapping into our intuition, that form authentic perspective. Let me share with you a few stories to add clarity to this idea.

A MIGHTY PERSPECTIVE SHIFT

I had just finished a talk to more than three hundred service women and men at a military training base. We had spent the afternoon talking about resiliency, mental toughness, and navigating emotional pain. An officer approached me and said he appreciated what I had to say and had been waiting to meet someone like me to ask a question. He wanted to know why he was "stuck." In my talk, we had explored the idea that sometimes when we get stuck on a point, that is a sign that there is an unresolved piece of information that needs to get stored differently.

The officer explained to me that he had served several tours of duty overseas during the last thirty years of his military career. He reflected that he had seen many things that the average person would not be able to bear. He had lost good people and knew first-hand the pain of war and service. The officer shared that on almost every tour, someone came home with not only physical injuries but emotional scars. He said these scars cannot be seen but can be felt by those who love them. "Maybe to everyone else these soldiers look fine, but their family will tell you they are not. Whether it be the nightmares, the short temper, or the thousand-yard gaze, their loved one who served never really came home." He went on to say that this is where he was stuck. "I lived through the same events as the other people who have been diagnosed with PTSD, but I don't have it. What's wrong with me, Doc?" he said. "Am I a heartless son of a bitch? I don't understand why some people get so messed up." Holding back tears, he said, "Why didn't I crack?"

We talked briefly about how he got into the military and why he stayed so long. He shared with me that after every tour and experience, he felt as though he grew stronger. His world views expanded. Every tour brought him more compassion and appreciation for life. He said every experience made him love his family more and recognize that being a soldier was his vocation. I observed that it sounded like while many others came home with post-traumatic stress, he came home with post-traumatic growth. It was as if time stood still. The noise of three hundred soldiers faded away in the background. This seasoned military officer looked at me as if I had just cracked a code. He nodded to me and took my hand. His large, weathered hand with visible scars dwarfed mine. With such care and tenderness, he said to me, "Yes, Doc, you're right. I chose to grow. I can't wait to get home and tell my wife."

When we come upon a truth, our mind, body, and soul align and our perspective is crystal-clear. Now, it is important to note that I am not suggesting that PTSD is a choice. In this example, the person connected with this framing or noting exercise of growth, and it felt true in his case.

A LITTLE BUT MIGHTY PERSPECTIVE SHIFT

Now, let's look at this from another point of view. Each fall, in local elementary schools across the province of Ontario, children participate in an event called cross-country running. With minimal training, students from grades three to eight take part in a race that is usually held at a local park or conservation area. The top finishers from each age group are invited to compete at the next level. As a working mom, there are times when my schedule does not allow me to get to some of our children's events, but I pick up the kids afterward.

One year, I let Ava know that I would pick her up at the end of the day from the park. When I arrived and saw Ava from a distance, my "mama sense" already knew that the day had not gone well. I could see her trying to hold it all together—she often bites her bottom lip as a strategy to keep in the tears. While I walked toward her, I started to think of what I could say to comfort her: "Darling, no one actually cares about cross-country running"; "This will never go on your résumé"; "You will still be able to get into a great school." These thoughts might have comforted me, but a ten-year-old, not so much.

Upon reaching Ava, I had nothing to say that I thought would bring her comfort, so I just hugged her as tightly as I could. In the safety of mom's embrace, all the emotions Ava had fought to keep at bay overcame her like a flood. I held my sobbing daughter in a parking lot. Through her gasps and tears she said to me, "Mama, I am so humiliated." As a mom and psychology person, I felt awful. I worry about the children who feel humiliation. That is the worst emotion for a child to navigate and the hardest to bounce back from. Humiliation leads to trauma. Humiliation breeds shame. And shame robs us of life itself. Supporting an angry or sad child is easier than trying to help a child who feels humiliated. All I could do was just keep holding her.

"Mama, I came in second place," she said.

My brain took a moment to register it. "Ava—are you kidding me? I thought this was something serious! For goodness' sake, I teach perspective, and clearly you have none!"

Ava pulled back and said to me, "My perspective is clear, Mama: I was the winner of all the losers today!"

I was speechless. I remember thinking in that moment, *Dear Lord, what have I done! How have I raised such a competitive, cutthroat child?* I made a mental note that Ava had no perspective and I would have to fix that later. But as many parents hopefully can relate, life picks up again, and you forget your child's lack of perspective!

A calendar year later, as the infamous cross-country race rolled around again, Ava was packing her bag for the day. The memory of the year before came back to me.

"Shoot. Ava, we never fixed your race perspective," I said to her over pancakes. "Let's have a wee chat about the difference between being a competitor and a participant. It is supposed to be fun. Don't take this too seriously and don't be too hard on yourself." I knew deep down that my words were evaporating, and Ava wasn't hearing any of it. She looked up at me with stone-cold eyes, and proclaimed, "Not this year, Mama. I'm taking this race down."

I started this story by saying that sometimes I must miss events, which usually hurts my heart. This event was different. I thought of it as a bright blessing that I had to teach at the university and could not watch the race. I actually didn't want to be there, because I thought Ava may knock over other children, and I didn't want to watch that!

At the end of the day, I collected Ava at the park just like the year before. This time, she was smiling and eagerly ran over to me. For a moment, I thought that I didn't want her to have won—I thought it was setting her up for a future of perfectionism and unsustainable standards. I decided it would be in her best interest to minimize the significance of a win so as to protect her from future hurts.

Not my best decision! As she jumped in my arms with pure jubilation, she yelled, "Today was the best day ever!" My response, which I am not proud of, was, "Really? People really care that much about cross-country running?" As soon as I said it, I knew I was giving Ava reason to attend therapy as an adult! I quickly apologized and asked her to tell me about her day.

Ava explained that it was amazing, and she was proud of herself even though she came in last place. Once again, my brain struggled to keep up. If you have ever wondered if psychology people know what they are doing with their children, I can assure you, we don't! All I could think of to say was, "Okay, tell me a little more about your day."

Ava explained that despite all her training and desire to win that race, she changed her plans on the fly. Another child who just happened to have special needs asked Ava if she wanted to run with her that day. Ava opted to run the race with this friend instead. "Mama, it was so special. We had a great run, and I let her finish ahead of me just at the last minute, so she wouldn't come last!"

Standing in that parking lot, listening to Ava recount her run, tears rolled down my face. She looked up at me and asked, "Mama, did I do the right thing? Why are you crying?" I replied, "Yes, Ava you did the right thing. That's perspective, girl, and I couldn't be prouder of you."

PERSPECTIVE IN ACTION

To me, perspective is the practice of mental nimbleness. We can be hungry for our goals. We can be focused and determined. But when called upon, we can shift our thinking quickly. It is also how we can prioritize what truly matters in the big picture. An example of this is when I was at a recent provincial meeting where we were discussing major changes to the educational landscape. People's roles were going to have to change and there was the possibility that we would have to rename certain positions. The positions would still exist, but titles and responsibilities could change. The anxiety in the room was very high and people were distraught about the idea of change. In that moment, I asked myself that question I always ask when change is on the horizon and fear seems to be running wild: "Is this change going to hurt my family?" I quickly recognized that it would not impact my family in any way, and the anxiety I felt melted away. A member of the group exclaimed, "This is going to kill the department and people are going to be devastated." I said out loud to the group quite abruptly, "No, this will not kill anyone." A woman asked me how I could be so calm about this idea of change in the workplace. I responded, "Because it is just that—work. We are not in any real danger."

Well, I might as well have been screaming into the wind with my three heads. Apparently, maintaining perspective in a room when others don't have much doesn't make you well liked.

Another example is the use of language and perspective. Take for example when people say things like, "OMG, this dessert is to die for," or "I would kill him if he ever did that," or "Arg, I have to go see my parents this Thanksgiving—the drive is brutal." To people who have experienced loss, death, and real-world trauma, this hyperbolic language is infuriating. Perspective is sharpened by loss and pain. Perspective is also formed by our value systems. Language matters. When people use emotionally charged language like the examples above, it contributes to an unspoken divide between people who have experienced trauma versus those who have not. As someone who has experienced trauma, you live your life as though you are not like everyone else anymore. You are different. There is an unseen divide between you and the world. More to come on this topic later.

PRACTICAL PERSPECTIVE

I am curious about how we can help support people in developing a solid sense of perspective without having to necessarily go through trauma, grief, pain, or loss. To address this we can look at the basic idea that as humans we are hardwired for struggle. We are meant to go through hard times. If it does not challenge us, it does not change us.

We are not meant to get through childhood or adolescence unscathed. Unfortunately, many parents think it is their duty to protect their child from everything. Of course, we must protect our children from real danger and threats. We need to take on the battles that they are not ready to tackle, but we must give them a chance to learn and grow as well. Author Barbara Coloroso, a respected professional speaker and consultant on parenting and teaching, writes that we must give our children the opportunities to learn how to make decisions that are age-appropriate. Her classic example for toddlers is the red or blue pyjamas question. She invites parents to ask their toddler, "Tonight at bedtime, would you like to wear blue or red pyjamas?"[1] It may seem overly simple, but toddlers who learn how to make age-appropriate decisions start to develop a trust within themselves. When I am in a room full of adults and no one can decide on where we should eat—"I don't know, where do you want to go?" "I don't know, where do *you* want to go?"—I laugh to myself and think, *If only your parent had let you pick your pyjamas, we would not be in this debacle!* We need to let our children make decisions, see natural consequences, and learn from them. A term we use in education is "failing-forward." We might have a setback, but that setback is a set-up for learning.

LEARNING PERSPECTIVE

Perspective forms as we age, and when adults are not given the chance to learn about consequences, they struggle. In education, we used to refer to one parenting approach as "helicopter parenting." This is when the parent system circles around the child, ready to jump in at the first sign of danger or difficulty. As an educator, I miss helicopter parents, since we now have a parenting practice known as "snowplough parenting," or, if you live somewhere warm, we can also call it "lawnmower parenting."

The idea here is that unlike helicopter parents, who swoop in when danger arises, snowplough parents clear a perfect path for their child so that the child is completely unaware there even is a problem. This creates a child who doesn't know how to problem-solve, make decisions, or learn from mistakes, and who usually lacks perspective-taking skills. Here is an example of a snowplough parent who had good intentions but was not doing their child any favours!

A dad called me and shared that he was gravely concerned that his son was going to be cut from a high-level basketball team on which he had played for two seasons. The dad was worried about how the rejection would impact his son. He asked me, a person who studies resiliency, what he should do. My heart went out to him. As a parent who has sat through many team-selection processes for multiple sports, I appreciated this dad's concern and acknowledged how difficult it is to watch your kids go through tryouts. As parents we feel helpless.

The dad also wanted to know how he could support his son with basketball if he lost his spot on the team. I told him all my sporting gems on resiliency. Michael Jordan didn't make his high school basketball team. Tom Brady went in the 199th spot in the NFL draft. I laid out a plan for that family and committed to supporting them through this. After a long pause, the dad replied, "Do you think if I sponsor the team, they will have to give my son a spot?"

SHARPENING PERSPECTIVE

As I've mentioned before, many people I have worked with who have sharpened their perspective share with me that it came to them after a great loss, hurt, or trauma. My intention to is help people foster perspective without having to go through such deep pain. I believe this is possible by cultivating empathy and compassion. We need to keep a humble heart. We can achieve this by being of service to others, and it is never too early to start.

Sheri Madigan and her colleagues from the Alberta Children's Hospital Research Institute write that parents and siblings can teach empathy by modelling how to value feelings; by connecting feelings, thoughts, and behaviours; and by building a climate of empathy in the home.[2] As adults we can also model these practices in our personal and professional lives. When a great tragedy strikes and we watch it on the news, we are often told to hold our loved ones closer or tell them how we feel before it is too late. Most of us pause and give an extra hug or call that person we love in the moment. But unfortunately, we fall back into the traps of being everbusy and taking for granted the people who matter most.

An important exercise to do to sharpen your perspective is to make a list of what matters most. A way to do this is an exercise called free-flow writing. Just get those ideas on paper. Don't judge—just jot!

- What are you grateful for?

- What can you not live without?

- What kind of person do you want to be?

- If someone was going to describe you in five words, what would those words be?

- What would you want those words to be?

We are quick to make to-do lists but rarely make "to-be" lists. Make your to-be lists. How do you want to be? As I navigated COVID-19 with my husband also working from home, plus three teenagers learning from home, two dogs, and three rescue cats, one of my "to-be" points every day was "be patient!" They needed a partner and parent who was calm and present, not wired and tired.

138 CALM WITHIN THE STORM

- Who do you want to be?

- How do you want to your children to remember their childhood?

Or

- How do you want to be remembered by your friends and family?

- What type of body do you want to live in? (Do you live now in a body of regret, hurt, and disappointment or a body of gratefulness, joy, and peace?)

It hurts my heart to see how many people live with the regret of not taking inventory of their life before tragedy strikes. "If only" are words I wish no person had to say.

I also find it reassuring that my jean size and cleanliness of my house are not likely to make my tombstone. And if for some reason they do, I give you permission to knock it over. Let's put our energy toward what actually matters. You don't want to end up saying, "If only I had spent as much time trying to help humankind as I had spent trying to lose the same ten pounds!"

As I tell my little tribe of five, the only thing I know for sure in life is that when I leave this world, I will leave loving them more than anything else.

HABIT-STACKING

It is helpful to build the practice of gratitude into your day. Gratitude is the antidote to anxiety and helps you maintain a clear perspective. You cannot reflect on your blessings and worries at the same time. The behavioural practice I

"When you change
the way you look at
things, the things you
look at change."

WAYNE DYER

recommend is called habit-stacking. James Clear has an amazing book on this topic: *Atomic Habits: An Easy & Proven Way to Build Good Habits & Break Bad Ones*; if you want to go further with the practice of habit changes, this book is the best in the field.

In short, here is the idea of habit-stacking: if you want to develop a new behaviour that will become a habit, pair it with a habit you already have. Here is an example: I am a devoted coffee drinker. It is a habit I do every morning without fail. No matter where I am in the world, my first order of the day is to find coffee. It does not even have to be good coffee! No one ever needs to remind me to drink coffee. No one says, "Tomorrow morning, Robyne, don't forget to drink coffee when you wake up!" It is a well-developed habit. Okay, maybe an addiction.

Now, if I want to change any behaviour or add a new behaviour, I need to habit-stack it with drinking my coffee. Each morning when I hold my coffee mug, that is the cue or trigger to remind me to practice my new behaviour. In this case, it is gratitude. With a warm cup in hand, I reflect on all the things that matter most. I express gratitude for my family, my health, and the opportunity to be of service to others, and I say my prayers. My coffee ritual has become my everyday Thanksgiving feast with far fewer dishes and less cleanup. I start my day focused on my blessings. I think it is fascinating that we will spend twenty minutes trying to find a show on Netflix but many of us struggle or cannot find the time to reflect and count our blessings! We can change that, though. We just need a few new habits in our arsenal!

What is the best habit you can use, and what can you stack with it that will help you maintain and keep perspective?

Perhaps the storms that have come into your life are not meant to destroy you, but rather to clear a path for something better. You cannot live a positive life with a negative mind. Perspective matters. The most readily available tool for keeping perspective is the practice of mindfulness.

66

Time does not heal—
acceptance does.

99

CHAPTER 8

ACCEPTANCE

BELOVED CANADIAN ACTOR Michael J. Fox, who famously played Alex. P Keaton on the TV show *Family Ties* and Marty McFly in the classic Back to the Future series, is a true champion of acceptance. Diagnosed with early onset Parkinson's disease in 1991, Fox is a testament to resiliency. In his book *Always Looking Up: The Adventures of an Incurable Optimist*, Fox writes about how tempted he was to pull away from everyone and suffer alone and in silence. When first diagnosed, he wanted to build walls to protect himself from the outside world. Instead, he learned the importance of fostering what he describes as an emotional, psychological, intellectual, and spiritual outlook that has helped him accept and thrive in his life with Parkinson's. Fox sums up acceptance so perfectly: "Acceptance doesn't mean resignation; it means understanding that something is what it is and that there's got to be a way through it."[1]

While working with people, including students, for almost two decades, the most common question I was asked was, "Why?"

"Why is this happening to me?"

"Why would he do that?"

"Why am I feeling this way?"

"We did everything right, but why did this happen?"

"They aren't good people, so why did they get that?"

This list could go on and on. Occasionally, someone would ask me a different type of question, and when it happened it always felt like a breath of fresh air! "Robyne, this is my story. How do I navigate this? What should I do? Who should I talk with? Where do I go?" I remember feeling a wash of relief when people asked me action questions. "Why" questions tell me you're stuck trying to make sense of the situation. I have seen people stay stuck in "why" questions for their whole life, never truly finding any answers. It is like the questions are trapped in an echo chamber. We go back to those questions when we are tired, overwhelmed, or depleted because they are like old friends—constantly there and easily accessible.

It is not a coincidence that the first academic departments were of ancient philosophy, and some may argue that philosophers are still asking the same "why" questions! This is because the questions let us sit with them. We philosophize; we ponder; we wonder; we imagine; we hypothesize. All of this thinking is wonderful, but we never really come to any definitive answers—and that can keep us stuck.

We also see big life questions here that keep us stuck, such as "What makes a good life?" Most of the go-to philosophers had opinions on that question! Aristotle believed it was our capacity to practice rational faculties. Socrates believed a good life was based on a person's ability to reflect on their existence and ask questions about the world around them. Plato argued the good life was spent in pursuit of higher knowledge and the obligation to the common good. Now, what is interesting to me is how that same question is asked of people in psychology. It takes on such a different direction. In psychology you would likely see a lot of responses that align with self-help ideas.

So, how do we get to the living part, beyond the thinking part? The answer: acceptance. The goal with acceptance is to move from "why" questions to action questions. Interestingly, acceptance in theory is simple, but the practice is not easy. It is helpful to remember that no amount of thinking about self-improvement will make up for a lack of self-acceptance.

Cognitive behaviourists talk about the importance of how we see the world, since that informs how we behave in the world. Within the field of cognitive behavioural therapy (or CBT) there is the practice of reframing or defusion. A simple example shows reframing using the power of language: If I tell my children they *have* to clean their room, their natural response is to feel resistance and disappointment. Few people tell their children they *have* to stop doing homework and go have fun. And even if we did tell our kids that they *have* to go have fun, say, at a party, the simple notion of being obligated to go and have fun makes the activity less fun!

If we change our language from "have to" to "get to," we ignite a sense of privilege and excitement. In practice, this could look something like: "I get to learn how to navigate my stress." The statement promotes curiosity, opportunity, and excitement because a potential solution is available to us. On the contrary, "I have to find a way to deal with this stress" creates more stress, anxiety, and even worry. You haven't been able to deal with it up to this point, so how likely is it that you will be able to now?

It is astonishing how quickly people find peace when they hear a new take or perspective on their challenge or difficult circumstance. This is one of the fundamental values of therapy. The therapist will mirror back to you what they hear, with perhaps a different emphasis, or with a few key details added. I love the "aha" moments, when all of a sudden you process information in a new way that breaks the chains of worry, fear, and shame, or when ideas burst through a newly opened window and you are flooded with relief and joy.

I sometimes actually get frustrated with myself that these moments happen in their own time! I wish they happened sooner. For instance, I was recently navigating a difficult situation at work, and I was feeling so mad that my brain and heart would not get on the same page. Intellectually I knew better, but my emotions were not cooperating. While driving home, I realized that if that situation hadn't been so challenging and difficult, I never would have considered leaving the job. If I had not left, I would not be writing this book! I needed that storm to create a new path I would not have seen otherwise.

Sometimes acceptance is elusive. When this is the case, we need to talk with others and find support. Therapy is a means of helping us find our way through the maze of "stuckness." A trustworthy person can help shine a light on what might be holding you back.

Another idea to consider regarding acceptance is that some people may not be ready to let something go and move on. I recall talking with a soldier who said that if he "got over" what had happened to him while he was on tour, he would be letting down his brothers who made the ultimate sacrifice. This soldier believed that his nightmares, fractured

"Most things will be okay eventually, but not everything will be. Sometimes you'll put up a good fight and lose. Sometimes you'll hold on really hard and realize there is no choice but to let go. Acceptance is a small, quiet room."

CHERYL STRAYED

relationships, and constant anger was his punishment for coming home alive. Another time, I talked with a parent who had lost her son. The mother shared that she felt enormous guilt and shame if she had a good day. Her negative self-talk would riddle her with accusations like, "What kind of mother are you? Your son is dead and here you are eating in a restaurant." This mother was plagued with maintaining her grief as a sign of loyalty to her son.

Just telling people to get over it will never work. We must understand the complexities that each story and experience carry for a person.

WE DON'T WANT A TEAM OF TOM BRADYS!

Now, not all acceptance challenges are related to loss. Some can be about how we see ourselves in the world. For this example, it is helpful to know that Tom Brady is an NFL quarterback who played with the New England Patriots for twenty seasons and won six of the nine Super Bowl championships he played in. He is a big deal, and the classic All-American-type football legend. This is hard to write as a loyal Dallas Cowboys fan, but facts are facts.

After I gave a talk on a military base, a young soldier asked if he could have a minute of my time. He said he wanted to know what to do when you can't accept something. He said directly, "I am never going to be okay with being five foot six—never, ever. My whole life I have been smaller, and I have worked harder than anyone else, but it doesn't matter."

The soldier shared with me that the pain of social comparison never left him—he was haunted by "always being the shortest dude in the room" and the names people called him. He was at the top of his class in military training and felt on top of the world for one brief moment, until he saw the picture. He said he looked like "a little kid" next to the other officers. "It is such a cruel joke the world plays on me every single day, Doc," he continued. "I can't think of anything else—I am just short AF."

Looking at this soldier, I was taken aback by the intensity of his anger directed toward his height. He looked relatively average height to me! I could see that this story he had written about himself was a constant narrative that created a vicious cycle. I took a deep breath. I nodded. I wondered how to best support him in that moment. I think sometimes people mean well when they offer support, but it actually makes situations worse. For example, I wondered how many people would say to him, "You're not that short! The average height in America is five foot seven—you're just an inch under. Get over it!" Or, "In boots, I am sure you're pushing five eight!" Most people just want others to stop being angry or in discomfort as quickly as possible because they're not okay sitting with those feelings. So when they try to appease the upset person, it is actually for their own benefit. But it is important to be real and acknowledge people's feelings, even when we don't agree.

In this case, I actually remember thinking, *With all the things a soldier could be worried about, you're worried about being short. Give me a break!* Of course, I didn't say that part out loud. Instead, I reflected to him the feelings I was hearing and seeing. I acknowledged years of frustration and anger about his height. I remember looking out at the sea of soldiers all around us and thinking that there were hundreds of examples of people in the room that weren't all the same size or shape. I asked my new friend if he liked football. He apparently was a New England Patriots fan. I asked him, "What if everybody on the team was the exact same size and shape? What if everyone was the exact build of Tom Brady, the quarterback? How would Tom Brady do as a centre or as running back?"

The solider laughed. He told me that despite Tom's impressive height (six foot four), the game would be a disaster. It would be awful if Tom played another position, he said.

So I asked him what it would be like if all fifty-five players on any NFL team were all the exact same size. What if every player—all 1,760 players across thirty-two teams—was exactly the same? He said that all the different sizes and positions were what made watching fun! A small nimble running back skirting around a huge linebacker. He said that if everyone was the same, it would be like watching robots. He said he wouldn't probably like it.

I explained to him that diversity is what makes things interesting. I asked him to reflect on what he could do well because of his size. The solider let out a great big laugh and through his smile said that since his arms and legs are shorter, he can do more push-ups and has less distance to squat than the others! We shared a hardy handshake and he went on his way. I don't know that soldier's name, but if he happens to come across this passage, I hope he knows that I think of him as a giant.

LIVING AN EXAMINED LIFE

At the heart of acceptance is the practice of living an examined life. We can't practice acceptance when we are not mindful. We need to tune into feelings, thoughts, and behaviours, as well as their respective impacts. We need to pause, take note, and reflect. I think many of us try to "do acceptance" on the fly, with dismal and scattered results. We put unrealistic demands on our heart to "just deal with this already." We are impatient and overly critical. Acceptance takes time. Compared with the way we heal physical injuries, we are not particularly skilled at healing emotional hurts. Parents whose children have mental health conditions have said that at times they wished their child had a physical injury instead. They say it would be easier to treat, and people would recognize that their child needed help and that the pain their child feels is real.

Another consideration is that we need to make time for working toward acceptance. We need to rest our emotions. Often, our attempt at acceptance is like trying to repair the treadmill when we are still running on it, in a full sprint! This isn't practical, or safe, for that matter. Acceptance is a process. It takes time, space, and intention. First, we need to commit to prioritizing our emotional health. Next, we set an intention. Then we map out daily practices that honour and support that intention. Eventually, like any other behaviour we do every day, this practice will become a habit, and that habit becomes our new outlook. And in time, the new outlook becomes one of the many habits in our behavioural repository of mastery. We may have to revisit our priorities every so often.

Those "why" questions are pesky and slip back into our thoughts. I see this especially when we are tired or over-whelmed. Pesky "why" question habits can also be triggered by more events that cause uncertainty. Eventually, with intention and commitment, we will start to spend less time wondering why and move forward. Journaling is an exceptional tool to support this practice. Research by James Pennebaker reports that journaling improves working memory since our brains are freed from the burden of holding everything in, and can help organize and process trauma.[2]

CALM WITHIN THE STORM

The act of journaling leads to clarity, which we need to start the acceptance process. A colleague recommended I try Julia Cameron's morning pages practice.[3] I was nervous at first, but this is a gem of an activity. The idea here is that every morning you write three pages of free-flow thoughts. I love the idea that you do this in the morning because, as Cameron explains, that's when the veil of the ego is said to be the thinnest. It is amazing to see how our days can change when we start with intention rather than on auto-pilot. If you are new to journaling, you may want to start with short writing bursts. I suggest starting with gratitude practices. *The Five-Minute Journal* (intelligentchange.com) is a gentle introduction. Or you can start by using just a Post-it Note to capture responses to these questions: What are you grateful for? What simple action can you take to express your gratitude?

I believe that gratitude is the antidote for an anxious heart. At nighttime, think of Bing Crosby's song "Count Your Blessings (Instead of Sheep)."

ACCEPTANCE IS A CHOICE

We cannot sit around waiting for the day we finally accept our life. We need to seek it out now.

I remember coming across this quote in a gym: "Being overweight is hard. Getting healthy is hard. Pick your hard." This rings so true for acceptance too. Staying stuck is hard. Acceptance is hard. Pick your hard.

Ultimately, acceptance is a choice. One day, you may want to make that choice, and when you do, you will be well equipped to start the "new hard" of moving to acceptance. There is no one clear path for this—you have to make it make

"We must let go of
the life we planned,
so as to accept the one
that is waiting for us."

JOSEPH CAMPBELL

sense for you. The most helpful approach I have come upon is to accept the present moment you are in right now, not the whole experience.

After the loss of a loved one, I carried the weight of all my grief for years after her death. On the fifth anniversary of her passing, I decided to get a memorial tattoo for her. I never expected this to be my first step of acceptance. But when I got it, the pain felt slightly lighter for the first time in five years. I now carried a sign of her on my skin, so my heart could finally have another spot to help share the load. I could remember how she lived, instead of ruminating on why she died. Please note, I am not recommending tattoos for all! Sharing this simply highlights that there is a path for everyone, but it's not the same path. Just look for the opportunity to take that first step. My tattoo reminds me that I need only to accept the present moment I am in. The present moment is really all we ever have. What accepting the now may look like at first is choosing to be stoic. It is choosing to practice mental discipline in that moment, so you do not go down a path that leaves you feeling lost and abandoned.

EMOTIONS AS TEACHERS, NOT ENEMIES

As a behaviourist, I am starting to realize that I have a wee bit of an issue with emotions! I like focusing on behaviours because we can count, measure, modify, and shape them. Emotions, on the other hand, are messy, unpredictable, fleeting, harmful, and glorious. They are hard to nail down. We love and hate them all at once.

As we think about acceptance, it is important to recognize the important role of emotions. People who have experienced great challenges have a tendency to feel "othered"—like they don't belong to the norm. The emotional piece is extremely difficult for people who have suffered trauma. Bessel van der Kolk, author of *The Body Keeps the Score: Brain, Mind, and Body in the Healing of Trauma*, is an amazing resource for people who need to go deeper into trauma acceptance. He writes that the goal is to make those horrific feelings and fear more tolerable, to create space for healing.

It is imperative that we acknowledge and recognize that emotional healing is as vital as physical healing. As such, emotional health is as important as our physical health. You matter. Your emotions matter. You are a whole person.

People who have experienced emotional trauma sometimes have experience echoes that are more difficult to process than the actual event. I believe that emotional regulation really helps here. Once the emotions are in scope, we can work on living with acceptance. There are a few techniques to get there.

Dialectical Behaviour Therapy (DBT)

One approach to working with our emotions and practicing acceptance is from the field of dialectical behaviour therapy.[4] An example of this theory in practice is radical acceptance. The goal of this approach is to change disruptive thought patterns and reframe them in a more helpful or positive way. Here is an example of this approach:

First write down the answers and then say them out loud. Revisit as often as is helpful.

- **State the event:** I was severely bullied in grade eleven.

- **State what caused the event:** I was new to the school. Did not fit in. I was perceived as an outsider.

- **State the feelings:** I get angry, hurt, and frustrated thinking about how other teenagers treated me. I am furious that teachers and administrators allowed this to happen. The adults at the school knew I was in danger and was being attacked. I am embarrassed and disappointed in myself that I did not fight back harder. I did not ask my parents for help.

- **State the plan:** This mixture of feelings is real, but it no longer serves me. I am choosing to move on. Holding on to these feelings continues to allow bullying and misbehaviour of adults to hurt me. Hate erodes the vessel it is carried in. I am choosing to acknowledge it happened and I am choosing to bring these emotions out of the shadows.

Emotions left unattended have a tendency to lead to stigma, so we want to meet our emotions with self-compassion and a non-judgemental lens. Research also demonstrates that we need to acknowledge both events and our interpretation of those events. We can acknowledge them to others or even just to ourselves. I love how Wendy De Rosa summed this up: "Healing requires you to feel your emotions, recognize your Ego carries a story and your Soul has the capacity to prevail through it all." [5]

Another common theme I see in this community is the importance of self-acceptance and self-forgiveness. Sometimes the greatest barrier to acceptance is not from the outside world at all—it is ourselves! We struggle to forgive ourselves, but an amazing power results when we finally do. This could very well be the hardest thing you do.

The season for feeling guilty has gone on long enough. Can you accept that you did the best you could at the time? Can you boldly state that you have learned something from those experiences? Do you see that carrying this any longer does not serve you? Are you ready to pick your hard? Regardless of any event in your past, you are here, and you matter, and so does your future.

"

We will never know
the full impact of what
being filled with hope can do
for ourselves and others.

"

CHAPTER 9

HOPE

DEPRESSION IS A disease that attacks hope. We do not talk about it like that, but I think it would be helpful if we did. To me, depression is when the body can no longer hold hope. I believe that deep in our sense of self, among the layers of life and story that make up who we are, there is a flame. Much like a pilot light, this flame is small but mighty. It is powerful and vital for keeping our heart engaged. It serves an important role in keeping the fire of our soul burning. When it is extinguished, hope is lost. And in that void of light, we feel empty, cold, and alone.

My life has been anything but linear. I have survived two episodes of when my flame went out. The world became dark and pointless, and I felt like I no longer belonged in it. I did not feel human anymore. My body and thoughts were strangers. Even breathing no longer felt automatic. Sometimes, sitting alone and staring like I was a million miles away,

I would catch myself gasping for breath. Even my automatic systems became effortful, and I had no effort to give.

I was institutionalized at sixteen years old, taken from a regular high school in the morning and admitted to a psychiatric hospital by late afternoon. A kind and seasoned school social worker named Kipp pulled the alarm. When Kipp saw me that day at school, she knew my pilot light had gone out and I was in real danger.

In Western society there is a tendency to treat emotional health problems very much like physical health problems: with medication. I do believe there is a role for medication in many forms of health and wellness, and that it can be used to give the body and mind the opportunity to stabilize and rest while we learn and develop new skills to manage our unique challenges. But for emotional health conditions, medicine ought to be only one part of the intervention. We need to treat the whole person. I needed to know that there was something on the other side of the pain, the bullying, the self-harm, and the shame. There was an impenetrable wall between the present day and a possible future. Life was an unsolvable puzzle. My sense of self was fractured beyond repair. All hope was gone. And in my particular case, the medication complicated my episodes because I did not take it consistently or correctly. Looking back, I think the treatment I needed most was rest, renewal, and a solid effort to regain hope.

I have held space for others in the darkest corners of despair, grief, and self-harm. I know this pain. Because of my time spent there, I am irrevocably changed. I acknowledge and believe in the pain of human suffering and honour everyone's experience in their own personal hell. If you tell me it hurts, I believe you. If you tell me your skin is ripping from the pull of grief, I believe you. If you tell me your chest is collapsing and crushing your lungs from the pain of help-lessness, I believe you. If you tell me you are never going to ever feel safe and okay again, I believe you. Whatever and however you feel is real. I believe you. And my intention here is to offer you a gentle invitation to explore the idea of reigniting that spark of hope. As your feelings are real, so is hope.

FINDING HOPE

So, how do we reignite that flame? How do we find and hold on to hope again when it has left us? How do we start believing again? Everyone experiences hope differently. From my work talking and sharing with people all over the Americas, I have hit upon a truth. As a scholar, there are very few times I can remember coming upon something with such clarity, confidence, and commitment that I knew it was significant beyond the present moment. Here's what happened.

As with most amazing life-turning moments, the day started like any other. I was presenting at a military base to hundreds of service members. After my talk, a group of soldiers approached me and shared that they had recently returned home from a tour. We talked casually at first, but the conversation turned more serious. They were curious about how they could support some of their colleagues who were not transitioning home that well. They themselves were doing all right, but other members of their division were struggling to reconnect with their family members. I asked them if they had done anything unique or different from the others to help prepare their own families for reintegration. They shook their heads and said there was nothing specific they could think of.

"Hope anchors the soul."

HEBREWS 6:19

One soldier seemed to think a little harder and then said the group had made promises that when, not if, they came home from their tour, they would finish all the household projects their partners could come up with! Another soldier said that he had gotten half of the kitchen painted before he left. Yet another laughed and said he had laid down most, but not all, of the hardwood floor in their living room. Each one shared a tale of some random project that they had to come home to finish. They all shared a laugh and the conversation wrapped up.

Shortly afterward, one of the senior members and I were talking. I asked him about how soldiers and their families reconnect after long absences. As someone who has studied attachment, I find this topic particularly impactful when we think about everyday resiliency. The senior officer shared that every member of the military probably has their own little approach to how they prepare and support their families before and after a deployment. I inquired about the soldiers I had spoken to earlier, who had house project lists waiting for them or had started projects before the deployment and left when they were only halfway done.

This weathered and hard-faced senior officer took a deep breath and nodded knowingly. "Doc, I believe those boys leave that as a sign of hope for their loved ones that they are coming back. Each day, their wife would see that half-finished project and say, 'He damn well better come home and finish this!'" He laughed softly and continued. "I wouldn't be at all surprised if some of those boys even had a pact that if someone didn't make it back, the others would finish the list for his brother!"

It was in that moment I came upon the truth: hope is a choice.

When we feel as though hope has escaped from our lives, whether because of disappointment, setbacks, loss, grief, or any other form of injustice, or perhaps even for no reason whatsoever, it is nearly impossible to trust that we will bounce back. What I learned from working with those troops was that even when the outcome of life is unpredictable, we always have a choice to make. We can choose hope. This is the heart of resiliency: believing and living hope-filled.

FOSTERING HOPE THROUGH TRANSFORMATIONAL THINKING

I believe the ultimate goal of hope is to create, foster, and protect a positive internal environment even in the presence of adversity, challenge, and setbacks. It is more than just optimism or blind trust. Many researchers have studied hope. Charles R. Snyder is considered one of the pioneers of hope research. His book *The Psychology of Hope: You Can Get There from Here* explains that hope is a motivational force that gives people the capacity to believe that they can experience positive outcomes by working toward goals. He believed that hope is the fuel that makes achieving your dreams possible. One approach for fostering hope comes from the practice of transformational thinking.

Let me explain. As we grow up, we develop an inner dialogue. This is sometimes called inner speech, verbal thinking, covert self-talk, or internal monologue or dialogue. Inner speech plays an important role in self-regulation and forming our sense of self in both toddlerhood and childhood, which we carry into adulthood. Some researchers say that our inner speech is actually a manifestation of how we were spoken to in our infanthood and childhood. Lev Vygotsky developed the model and the current understanding of inner speech supports this idea.[1] How you talk to your children will eventually become their internal dialogue. Other researchers have concluded that private speech is a universal phenomenon, crucial for personal development. Therefore, every human being has varying degrees of inner speech. This marvel of being able to have a conversation with ourselves is an invaluable skill for self-regulation, motivation, and performance. Our inner speech is closely interconnected with our thoughts.

In my opinion, that thinking self is one of life's greatest mysteries despite all that we know about our cognitive functioning and capacity. Our inner thinker is a fickle friend. Somedays the inner dialogue is supportive, encouraging, and extremely helpful; however, other days that inner thinker is mean, cold, vengeful, and destructive. We will never truly understand the battles some people engage in daily. It is like a personal civil war or a never-ending game of tug-of-war. I believe that these complex systems, the inner speech and our inner thinker, are responsible for holding and fostering hope. When there is a breach or decline in our personal hope, we need to pay special attention to making repairs. Personal relationship repair is often challenging because we are quicker to forgive others or give them the benefit of the doubt than we are ourselves.

How we can finally address all these mental pushes and pulls is through the practice of transformational thinking. Transformational thinking is overcoming the limits that we have imposed upon ourselves. It is creating a consciousness that will set us on the path of achieving the results to which we aspire. It is connecting with the core of who we are and knowing our value. It is rebuking the inner speech that does not serve us. It is no longer asking our emotions permission to be who we want to be.

Tools for Choosing and Building Hope

To develop transformational thinking, which is what we need to foster hope, we need to first listen to and recognize our inner dialogue. We need to change our thinking. Our thinking is directly related to our capacity for hope. Acceptance and commitment therapy, or ACT, has many tools that can help here. (For more information, check out *ACT Made Simple: An Easy-to-Read Primer on Acceptance and Commitment Therapy* by Russ Harris.) You may wonder what ACT has to do with hope. The answer lies in the notion that hope is a choice. Therefore, using ACT, we can start practicing and incorporating behaviours in our lives that foster hopefulness as part of our value system, and commit to action while being more hopeful. Here is a summary of some of the key ideas that you can use to finally let go of that rope in the mental game of tug-of-war!

Turning Inward: Contact with the Present Moment

First, we want to set the intention to spend some time every day turning inward. Check in with your thinking daily, whether it be through meditation, reflection, or journaling. Take a few minutes every day to listen inward. The aim is to transition from the outer world to the inner world.

We have the time—we just need to prioritize ourselves. One way to start this practice is through mindfulness. I like to think of mindfulness as paying attention to our thoughts on purpose. Ask yourself: What am I thinking about right now? Take the time to listen to and observe your thoughts. Regardless of what you come upon in terms of your thinking and self-talk, meet those observations without judgement. We are particularly susceptible to falling into thinking patterns that are either regretting the past or worrying about the future. We spend little time in the present moment if we are not intentional about it. The world moves quickly. There is a lot of noise. Most of us are just trying to keep up. Although practicing mindfulness is challenging at first because automatic thinking is so prevalent, the more we practice, the better we become at turning inward and listening to our thoughts.

A common misconception about mindfulness is that we have to practice it in stillness. The reality is that you can practice mindfulness anywhere and anytime. A study from Florida State University about mindful dishwashing yielded interesting results. The students were divided into two groups prior to taking on the task of washing dishes. Group 1 was read a short passage about mindfulness and being present in the act of dishwashing. It encouraged the students to notice the temperature of the water, the bubbles, the movement and flow of the water, and feel of the plates in motion. The other group was presented a brief paragraph on the importance of dishwashing and hygiene. The researchers found that the students who had participated in mindful dishwashing reported an increase of 25 per cent in feeling "inspired" and a decrease of 27 per cent in feelings of nervousness compared with the other group.[2] The researchers concluded that being mindful and aware in even mundane tasks could actually support a positive state of well-being. This finding is important because a positive state of well-being allows hope to grow.

Another example is mindful walking in nature. You can mindfully walk indoors as well, but being outside carries added benefits. Adam Brady writes that being in nature serves us in six ways:

1 It connects you more deeply with the environment.
2 It gets you out of your head.
3 It helps you get to know your body.
4 It slows you down.
5 It increases your intentionality and awareness.
6 It makes space for mindfulness.[3]

Simply set the intention that you are about to take part in a mindful walk. Start by standing still (yoga mountain pose). Feel your feet firmly on the ground and create a strong back with an open heart, facing forward. Take your first step into nature, paying specific attention to your foot making contact with the earth and your breath flowing naturally in and out. Continue this way, paying attention to your body and everything around you. Enjoy!

Cognitive Defusion

The second area of focus within ACT is the notion of cognitive defusion. This is the practice of reducing your attachment to your thoughts. I observe so often that people believe their thoughts to be solid truths—if I am feeling it or thinking it, it must be real or true. Please remember that while whatever we are feeling is real, as I said at the beginning of the chapter, the feelings do not have to define us. Feelings are not who we are. The main idea of defusion is putting space between your thoughts and your reality. For example, I could say, "I am anxious and that translates into me being an anxious person." Conversely, I could say, "I am noticing I am having anxious thoughts, but the thoughts do not make up an identity. My core—my identity or my self—notices something there, but it is not permeating the essence of who I am."

Acceptance

The third area of ACT is the practice of acceptance. Acceptance, as we discussed in chapter 8, is simple in theory but hard to do. The heart of acceptance within ACT is the notion that "what you resist, persists." The harder we try to ignore, push away, or avoid feelings or thoughts, the stronger they become. The acceptance of emotions and thoughts here is about creating an internal environment in which they can coexist. A popular example in ACT to illustrate this idea is that of holding a small cactus plant in your hand. The harder you squeeze it, the more painful the experience. A light touch is less uncomfortable. So, hold those thoughts and feeling gently.

Self as Context

For the fourth element of ACT, we are challenged to reframe how we see ourselves. A friend of mine, Fergal O'Hagan, is an extraordinary professor of human behaviour. He finally helped me truly understand this concept. Like many people, I thought my sense of self was actually made up of all the thoughts, feelings, memories, and experiences I have ever had. My identity was fused to the thoughts and feelings.

O'Hagan introduced me to the notion of "self as context" and explained that who we are is the core of our identity, but that is not made up of feelings and thoughts. The self is actually the part of us that can *observe* the thoughts and feelings. Putting space between our core and the part of us that recognizes that core is how we can gain a greater perspective and build capacity for seeing more clearly, without being defined or held down by thoughts and feelings.

Values-Driven Living

The fifth component of ACT resides in our values. This is where we develop an awareness of what we value and use those values as a compass to guide our behaviours. In order to understand the practice of values-driven living, it is helpful to differentiate values from goals.

Goals are things we strive for—finishing a degree, saving for a vacation, or maybe having dogs that don't go bananas when the doorbell rings (Luna and Apollo need work here).

Values are the core of what we believe. What matters most in the big picture? Russ Harris, the developer of ACT, asks these questions to help bring clarity to your values:

- What really matters to you, deep in your heart?
- What do you want to do with your time on this planet?
- What sort of person do you want to be?
- What personal strengths or qualities do you want to develop?[4]

Values are a way of identifying what matters to you in an actionable outcome. Values can include:

- Authenticity
- Compassion
- Connection
- Faith
- Family
- Flexibility
- Freedom
- Gratitude
- Health
- Hope
- Industriousness
- Love
- Loyalty
- Order
- Persistence
- Resiliency
- Skillfulness
- Supportiveness
- Trust

This list is by no means exhaustive, but it helps you think about who you are and what matters most. I encourage you to write down five values. Sometimes people share that they feel distance between what values they hold and what their reality looks like. They report that their values are inspirational but not possible in the everyday busyness of life. They want to be flexible or easygoing but they feel like they are rigid, brittle, and demanding.

It is important to recognize these inconsistencies in our lives but not hold on to them too tightly. Recognize that there are occasions when we are pulled in the opposite direction of our value base. The intention is that you start each day being more mindful of your values and make the decision to act more closely in line with the desired value rather than regressing to the habit you may have. It is a choice, every day, to live a values-directed life. When a decision is on the horizon, plan based on what is most aligned with your values.

Commitment

The last component of the ACT model is commitment. This is when you commit to acting in a manner that supports your values. You identify a goal that connects to your value and you choose behaviours that bring you in that direction. For example, if your value is health, then you plan what healthy practices you will adopt. For example, start by walking each day for thirty minutes. Rain or shine, busy or on vacation— you commit to walking thirty minutes each day. You set that behaviour as a priority and you honour it as often as you possibly can. You can even set the goal of walking a minimum of 80 per cent of the days this month. So, for the month of January, you are going to walk at least twenty-five days. The other six days are flex days. One of the most common errors we make when we start adopting new behaviours is trying to do too much too quickly, and we stall out. Think about New Year's resolutions. According to an article in *Forbes*, research from the University of Scranton shows that less than 10 per cent of goals are ever met.[5] That stat is even lower if it is tied to a New Year's resolution. In his podcast *Champion Minded*, sports author Allistair McCaw states that it is important to focus on one behaviour at a time and set the intention to consistently work on that behaviour for ninety days for it to really become part of you. McCaw landed on the idea of ninety days based on his work supporting athletes across sports. He interestingly notes that unfortunately, it takes only nine days to lose the habit![6] Research from the University College London found that it took it approximately sixty-six days to learn and keep a new habit.[7] So, it looks like it might be a wee bit longer than the twenty-one-day promise many people and products proclaim.

LESSONS OF HOPE

As our children entered preschool, I had a stark realization about my parenting. Every time any of the children attempted something that required increased independence, such as going outside to play or walking to a friend's house just a few doors away, I gave my permission alongside a fearful warning: "Sure, you can walk to Emy's house, but be careful about cars. They won't be looking for you since they are all texting and driving"; "Yes, you can play basketball out front, but watch out for strangers and odd cars. Be sure to come to the front steps if a car pulls up or a stranger walks by—come get us

"This process of the good life is not, I am convinced, a life for the faint-hearted. It involves the stretching and growing of becoming more and more of one's potentialities. It involves the courage to be. It means launching oneself fully into the stream of life."

CARL R. ROGERS

immediately"; "Yes, you can have a sleepover, but remember last time, you came home with a hangover from the lack of sleep and sugary treats." Every time our children tried to spread their wings just a little, I gave them more detailed warnings about the dangers of our world! Now, as parents we want to protect our children, of course, but I observed that in all my attempts to support them, I was sending the message that the world is dangerous.

I believe that we need to temper our "beware" and "have fun" messaging. Trying to prevent them from experiencing danger or hurt can sometimes have the opposite effect. They lose hope that the world is a wondrous place. As we think about everyday resiliency, the practice of living hopefully despite the potential of hurt and risk is a crucial skill for children to learn. Again, I get that as parents we want them to be safe, but not too safe for their own good. It is a fine line between being a supporter and being a rescuer for our children.

SEEING HOPE FROM A CHILD'S POINT OF VIEW

Hunter was playing in the championship game of a provincial basketball tournament, and his team was behind by a point with only seconds left in the game. The atmosphere in the arena was wild. Parents from both teams were on their feet cheering for their players. The opposition had the ball and were working their way down the court. Out of nowhere, Hunter was able to anticipate a pass and forced a turnover. He had a wide-open lane and went for a classic layup. The layup is always the smart choice, I would tell Hunter. Be sure to go for great scoring chances, not just good chances. "Pick great shots, not good shots—Mama, I know," he would say.

The parents and supporters of our team exploded into cheers and celebration as the game clock ended. Hunter's team piled on top of him, and parents in the stands were hugging me too. This was a big day for our boys.

But as we celebrated, a frantic referee was blowing his whistle. He was waving his arms. He was signalling no basket. He called a foul. He called Hunter for travelling. On a wide-open layup opportunity, Hunter had taken an extra step. The basket didn't count, and no time remained. The other team had won. It was now time for the opposition to celebrate. I think their celebration was even greater, since they went from defeat to victory within moments. That is a lot of ground to cover!

Our team headed off the court, their disappointment palpable. My heart dropped for Hunter. I knew how this was going to play out: he would see it as his fault that his team had lost the championship. As a parent, sometimes the most difficult feeling we must navigate is utter helplessness. There was nothing I could do. I was also disheartened that some of our team's parents commented to me that Hunter should have known better; he should have been more careful. Thankfully, I was more interested in getting to my son than starting a brawl in the stands with those parents.

Through the sea of people and celebrations, I finally found Hunter. He was still standing under the basket. His forehead was scrunched up, as it gets when he is trying to figure something out and is giving it his full attention. We found each other's eyes. I got the little nod; it was okay to make contact. All my years as an educator, counsellor, and therapist did not provide me with the words I desperately needed in that moment. I decided I would say nothing and hold space for Hunter to take the lead. He could say anything or nothing, and I would just hold space for him—whatever he needed.

Hunter looked at me and said, "Mama, that hurt. I'm sorry that happened, and I feel like I let my team down. But you know what, now I know what losing a championship feels like. I hope I get a chance to feel what winning one is like. I want to win a championship for my team. I want to make that shot. I hope that will happen one day."

Our children are our greatest teachers. That day, Hunter taught me that we have the power to choose one thought over the other. On the court, he went through the event and chose to find hope over his disappointment, to look forward and see the potential rather than look back at the past and get stuck in regret.

In Hunter's first year of high school, and at his first championship, he led the team in scoring and helped bring home the high school district championship title. It took five years and a lot of practices, games, and coaching, but Hunter finally experienced his championship. When he ran into the stands, he picked me up and gave me a big hug. He put me down gently, leaned in, and whispered, "I didn't get called for travelling once that game!" What Hunter hoped for, he worked for, and it came to him.

Those who know me know I am the eternal cheerleader for the underdog. I am also a wee bit of a fixer. Those two combined can be trouble; it requires strong boundaries. A few years back, I set the intention to take a step back from my volunteer work, including coaching sports, so I could spend more time at home. (Looking for that ever-elusive work–life balance!) On the very day I made this silent commitment, Jaxson came home and told me that his basketball team was not going to play this season because they could not find a coach. The team was small, and no one was interested in coaching them. As I started explaining to Jaxson that I needed to pull back from coaching, he said, "And they said we couldn't ask a mom to coach because moms are girls and girls don't know anything about basketball. Mama, this is my team. This means I won't be able to play."

Well, Jaxson was holding my kryptonite in his little hands: it was a group of underdogs; a problem needed solving; there was clearly a social justice issue; and this was all impacting my littlest cub, Jaxson. Mama Bear was in.

It is important to note that basketball is actually not my first sport. But I had spent most of my childhood and adolescent years as an athlete: I had great success provincially and nationally in figure skating, and later coached teams to provincial rankings. Thankfully, NCAA coaching credentials are transferable, so I had the requirements to step up as coach for Jaxson's team.

Soon, we had our first practice. The season was chock full of ups and downs, challenges and frustrations, and clearly a heavy dose of sexism. Some people really don't like women coaching boys. I saw this from parents of my own team, from other teams, and even from other coaches and referees. A few of my players told me that their dads had said they did not have to listen to me because I was just the team babysitter. That felt good! I took those moments to talk about respect and the importance of gender equality. I think it is highly likely that this was the first time some of these boys heard that lesson. I also said a silent prayer for their mothers and sisters—how hard must it be for women who live in those types of relationships. That season, I realized I was somewhat insulated from the negative attitudes of others about women in sport, since I spent most of my time with likeminded people who celebrated and protected equality. Nevertheless, I saw a negative side of the sport I love. I had to make a choice.

Instead of getting hurt and frustrated, I chose to hope that I could set a new example for my players. I had little support from the families and organization, but I leaned into my beliefs, values, and expertise as a coach. I knew I could coach this team. And I knew I had the opportunity to break down stereotypes and inequity, and that it was an honour to do so. And when I had those moments, when I was ready to throw in the towel and hand my whistle to those dads standing in the corner of the gym during practice, drinking triple-triple coffees and critiquing my every move, I focused on Jaxson's face. He loved that I was his first rep coach. He told me that every day.

That group of parents seemed to have a change of heart when my wee team of underdogs went undefeated in the Ontario Basketball Championship weekend. Here we were, going into the gold medal game, undefeated and favoured. As my players took the floor, each of the boys stopped and wrapped their little arms around my waist. I had gone in for a high five, but they met me with a hug. One player said to me, "I love that you are my coach. I love basketball again." He was the son of the most difficult dad. Another player said, "I love that we are here with a mom coach! How cool is it that Jaxson's mom knew that we could make it here even before we did."

Hope is not only a choice, it is also contagious. Show others what you hope for them. Tell others what you see as their capabilities. Be brave enough to hold hope through adversity. Box out hard those people who say otherwise.

Now, I wish I could tell you my team won that gold medal. That we all had our moment, like in a Disney movie when a team of underdogs come together, against the odds, and win. When the game buzzer went off, we were down by only one point. As my team was awarded their silver medals, I wondered if they would still take the lessons I had tried to impart that season.

As I was packing up my coaching bag and the gym was almost all cleared out, Jaxson walked up to me with the biggest smile on his face. (His smile is a direct line to my heart.) I was happily surprised that he seemed to be okay with the loss. It was a hard-fought game, and he had played well. He was a brilliant teammate and took the loss with grace, poise, and sportsmanship that outweighed his age. He had left it all on the court, and I couldn't have asked him for anything more. From behind the smile, he let out a little laugh. He said, "Mama, we lost by one point, just like Hunter did five years ago, in the same tournament! That means my championship is waiting for me too, in high school." As I held Jaxson, I echoed his idea in my heart. I hope so too, Jaxson. I hope so too.

Choose hope in everything you do. It matters. We will never know the full impact of what being filled with hope can do for ourselves and others.

"

Remember: motivational quotes
won't work unless you do!

"

CHAPTER 10

HUMOUR

W HEN I FIRST started researching, thinking, and writing about resiliency, the last pillar of my baseline for resiliency eluded me. I recognized the variable as a common trait among the hundreds of people I met and worked with, but I didn't know what to call it. I didn't know how to operationalize it. And since I couldn't define it clearly or package it in a simple word, I kept omitting it.

For a while, whatever that fifth pillar was, I began thinking of it much like Lord Voldemort from the Harry Potter series— "the fifth element of my theory that cannot be named!" Calling it "light-hearted," "capacity for fun," or "seeing the bright side," felt too simplistic, and not clear. Because of the reality of the true pain and hurt that accompanies so many of us in our lives, it also felt too dismissive to attach a fluffy or soft title to the big picture of resiliency. I was also worried that it would be taken out of context, that people could misread "humour" as just "suck it up, buttercup" or "lighten up!"

In 2015, I was asked to do a TED Talk on resiliency. I had always wanted to be someone who had done a TED Talk (please notice the past tense). The prospect of doing a TED Talk in the future, though, was a different story. I felt a combination of terrified, excited, bewildered, and at a loss for words exactly when I needed twenty minutes' worth of words! I was still struggling to appropriately identify and incorporate the fifth pillar of the baseline for resiliency. With time ticking away, I went ahead with only the four, but I regretted not being able to present the model with all five parts. If you happen to watch that TED Talk, you will see I eluded to humour, and shared a little story, but moved on quickly since I didn't have this idea crystallized yet.

On reflection, I know that I held another concern about including humour. I worried that people would think I was saying there is a silver lining in everything, or that laughter is the best medicine. I do not believe there is necessarily an unseen benefit in everything, and while laughter does benefit us physically in terms of health (more on this below), I think antibiotics are the best medicine for bacterial infections! Life's pain and daily stress is more complicated than the simple idea of laughter. When life is awful, and no-good, rotten things happen, I hope you will find people who will stand next to you and *not* say, "It is all in the greater plan." I want people to hold space for you and say, "This is awful and it sucks!" You don't need someone who tells jokes or makes light of it. If I was standing with you, I would say, "I see that you are hurting, and I believe you. I will hold space for you to say and do anything you need to do or say, without judgement or offering trite little sayings about it being for a greater purpose, or that these things were meant to happen. I won't make light of it or tell you it is okay. Because sometimes, my friend, it simply is not okay."

So, here was my dilemma. I recognized something in people who showed enormous amounts of resiliency beyond the other four pillars, but I still couldn't put a label on it. I wanted a word that could summarize and honour this significant capacity of not taking oneself too seriously and the ability to hold space for self-compassion, self-love, with the fun, the funny, and all the other light-hearted and tender things, despite the stressors, hurt, and pain.

What I have hit upon since is that just because we don't know exactly what something is, it doesn't mean it doesn't exist or matter or shouldn't be included. So, I finally landed on the word: humour. And when I say humour, I mean it in the most inclusive, broadest-sweeping kind of way. Humour is a constellation of joy, play, not taking yourself too seriously, seeing true beauty, having a sense of awe and wonder, and having your wits about you. It is being able to say fifteen WTFs in a single day and keep going! This kind of humour can hold just enough space in the face of a challenge, crisis, or hurt for a little sunshine to peek through. It is when you can take that final straw—you know, the one that will break the camel's back—and choose to laugh out loud at the absurdity of your life instead . . . because the alternative is brokenness with no relief in sight.

MY CONSTELLATION OF HUMOUR: WHERE TO BEGIN?

Mark Twain said, "Humor is the great thing, the saving thing. The minute it crops up, all our irritations and resentments slip away and a sunny spirit takes their place."[1] That sums it up quite well! Humour is a way of loosening up the grip life has on us. In the spirit of my definition of humour being a whole bunch of ideas wrapped into one, I want to break down a few of the key elements.

Laughter

The science of laughter is actually funny. Many scientists believe that laughter is a social emotion that we use to create and maintain bonds with other people. It is also an extremely primitive way of making sounds. Researchers have identified laughter as universal: when laughter is broken down, it forms sounds like "ha-ha," "ho-ho," or "hee-hee," all of which make up the universal human vocabulary and can be produced and recognized by people from different cultures.[2] It's safe to say that laughing has been around for a very long time!

Laughter is also present in animals, which is fascinating. Almost all mammals play when they are young and produce sounds that can be traced to laughter. Some mammals, like otters, rats, dogs, and cats, can carry play into adulthood and produce laughter-type sounds. Laughter is extremely important because for all species, it signals play, and more importantly, it typically signals that no one is going to get hurt in this present moment.

Another amazing fact about laughter is that it is the body's natural painkiller. Researchers found that when a person genuinely laughs, their body releases endorphins. According to Robin Dunbar and his colleagues at the University of Oxford, laughter reduced a hospital patient's need for opioid painkillers, and interestingly, the positive effect of laughter seemed to last even after the laughter stopped. Overall, patients responded better to subsequent pain episodes as well. The Oxford researchers' work includes the finding that laughter amps up your immune system too. Other researchers have found similar results. In the short term, laughter stimulates your organs, since you are taking in more air; activates and releases your stress response; and soothes away built-up tension. In the long term, laughter has been found to improve your immune system by releasing neuropeptides that help fight stress buildup; relieve pain in the moment and increase your pain threshold; increase your personal satisfaction with relationships and social bonds; and improve your mood.[3]

So, how do we get more laughter? First, set the intention to look for it. Instead of watching that World War II or tear-jerker movie (these have a place too, but we will talk about that later), look for a comedy. You can also try looking up jokes. Be sure the laughter you are seeking out is not at the expense of another person or an animal. (It is important to know what is and isn't funny. Use your judgement. A way to do this is to ask yourself if the joke or funny show aligns with your values.) Another practice is to solicit the help of funny people, especially children. Our littlest, Jaxson, is a master of jokes. I have seen that kid drop a joke and make a room full of adults bend over laughing. When an adult asked Jaxson how he became so funny, Jaxson replied, "I'm third-born, there is no photo evidence of me as a baby—I need to make sure people remember me!" (Before you start judging us as parents, please know there are plenty of photos of Jaxson! They may not be in a baby book like those of his siblings, but they are safely stored on a memory stick for whenever he wants them!)

The idea here is to build laughter into your world. Again, this is not in the moment of crisis, per se. It is in the other parts around it. Some of the most precious memories I have of loved ones who have died are of their faces, their laughter, and reminiscing over shared experiences of joy. I protect these memories at all costs and hold them deep in my heart. Your moments of laughter and shared joy can bring an indescribable sense of comfort and closeness when you are apart. I can still see, feel, and hear my mother's laughter and smile. I know while she was here with us, and we were together, we lived it up and had fun. Those happy memories bring moments of relief from the grief and sadness.

When you are living with grief, it feels like you will never laugh again or be able to find joy. But you will in time. Unlike many popular opinions that suggest that you will eventually "get over" the grief, time will not heal, but you will learn how to hold space for your grief at the same time as holding space for new experiences. Grief becomes part of your bones. It lives in every cell in your body. You will learn how to carry it with you. You may even want to. I want to keep my grief; I want to take it with me everywhere, because it is my last connection to my mother and reminds me how important our relationship is.

Eventually, there will come a day when grief and laughter can coexist. And it will not feel like you are disrespecting your loved one by being able to laugh or have fun. That first moment of laughter will feel like the sun breaking through the darkest day. It will remind you that life is made up of an astronomical number of events, experiences, and emotions that all work together to form our stories. If you are hurting right now, my hope is that this day is close for you. I want you to find that place where grief and good can coexist.

I vividly remember the first time I laughed again after my mom died. It was little Jaxson who brought the much-needed, momentary relief. Jaxson and I were walking up the steps to daycare, and he stopped to look at a snowman that children had made the day before. "Mom, do you know what the snow smells like for a snowman?" he asked. In my fog, I didn't give it much thought. "No, Jax, I don't know," I said. Jaxson pulled my arm so I looked at him. "Carrots—the snowman thinks the snow smells like carrots!" He fell to the ground laughing so hard at his own joke. He was rolling around, holding his sides, and little tears were streaking down his cheeks. Jaxson held open the window, just ever so slightly, for me to see the sun rising again. And I have never looked at a carrot or snowman the same way again.

Play

Somewhere between childhood and adulthood, many of us stop playing. As adults, with the competing demands of work and family, our leisure time is usually spent zoning out in front of screens or sleeping. However, just as play is extremely important for childhood development, we need to play as adults too. The research on adult play is convincing. Play helps fuel creativity, imagination, and problem-solving abilities, which are extremely important for "adulting." Research also reports that adult play relieves stress, improves brain function, boosts creativity, supports mindfulness, enhances relationships and connections with others, and keeps us young and energized.[4] Now, if there was a pill you could take or a class you could attend that could do all that, people would be signing up in droves to take part. The benefits of play almost sound too good to be true. But the reality is that these are the benefits when we carve out time for play!

For starters, just try sitting on the floor again. See your world from a different vantage point. Go outside, dribble a ball, build a snowman, colour, paint, throw the ball for your dog, or jump in a puddle. Really, anything goes at this point.

The important part to remember is that it doesn't always have to be structured and organized. It can be a little chaotic, messy, and unplanned, and that's usually where we find the greatest benefits.

Play can also be thought of as a state of mind. Stay curious, open, and adventurous. Foster and nurture your playful side. All of us have a playful side; we are born with it. We learn so much through our drive for play. Some people may have had to let go of that part of themselves earlier than others, but we can find it again. It is just one big puddle jump away!

A parent recently shared with me that they tried to get their teenager to go outside and play, and their teenager offered the parent another place they could go. The parent walked away from the insult and went outside and started dribbling a basketball and taking shots. Usually the parent and the teenager would get into an argument. Instead, the parent chose peace and play. ("Peace" and "play" were their words of focus for the month that we had mapped out.) The parent did not engage the teenager and the disrespectful behaviour, but rather reflected and recalled how important play is for them as an adult, and remembered their focus words. After about fifteen minutes, the teenager came out, gave a remorseful apology, and asked the parent if they wanted to play 21.

This is what parental resiliency looks like. A teen might feel justified in being disrespectful when their parent engages their bad behaviour or retaliates, because that behaviour is also out of line. But in this case, since the parent did not react, the teenager had to sit with the last word, and that last word was not cool. The parent chose peace and play instead of fighting, and eventually their teenager joined them. This is the outcome we strive for. I think as parents we have the power to set the example. Keep doing you and make time for play. It is amazing how quickly others will come and want to play too!

Finding Joy

When Ava was in grade two, she was frantically looking for something lost in my room. I came in to see if I could help her. She looked up at me and said, "Mama, I was trying to find your joy for you. I heard you tell Grandpa you lost it. What does it look like?" The innocence of children stops me dead in my tracks every time. Again, our children are our greatest teachers. After a particularly difficult season in our lives, which had *no* silver lining, I was left feeling numb. I was going through the motions but was not really present. I could hold a million-mile-away stare and think of absolutely nothing. I spent so much time trying to compartmentalize emotions, I felt nothing. So, how do you start to find joy again? Great question. For me, it started with a seven-year-old girl trying to find it on my behalf.

Much like with laughter and play, we need to set the intention for finding our personal joy. Joy looks different for everyone. I invite you to make a list of things that bring you unique and blissful moments of joy. You could look online for examples or ask other people about their joy, but I think that sometimes those lists are too general. Create one that is more reflective of you. You know you better than anyone else. When I read other people's suggestions for joy, although they sound lovely, they are not necessarily for me. "Take a long walk on the beach," for example: No beaches are really near me so long drives are involved, and at best we have only three or so months a year of beach weather. Despite enjoying the beach in general, parts are not joyful for me—carrying all the gear, seagulls looking for handouts, and sand in my car afterward. Oh, and the sunburns as a fair-skinned, freckled redhead! This doesn't make me feel joy! Neither does the suggestion to read a book in the bath—has anyone really figured out how to turn the page with wet hands? Do anyone else's children bang on the door looking for soccer socks if you are in the bath for more than five minutes?

I think you get the idea here. Do *you*, not what other people say you ought to do or like. Remember, everyone is different and that is the beauty of this. Joy is your personal mosaic that reflects your truest sense of yourself. Just to show you how every list is unique, here are a few things that bring me joy.

- Getting a car wash. I always say, "Ahhh" out loud as I drive out.

- Drinking a flat white coffee anytime. Sometimes, I actually hug my cup as an expression of gratitude for the joy this drink brings to my life!

- Walking my dogs at sunrise, when I am wearing snow pants and it is freezing out! (See? This probably would not end up on an internet list for joy!)

- Cleaning my house with music playing.

- Sitting on old, smelly high school bleachers watching my boys playing basketball—the older the school gym, the better!

- Doing Ava's perfect bun hair before a gymnastic competition and watching that bun stay put for the whole meet.

- Opening a new book and reading the first sentence. I imagine how much thought the author put into that first sentence.

- Making a plan. Plans bring me joy!

- Working out: a run, yoga class, walk—joy is one workout away!

- Working on projects with my husband. Any project with Jeff is joyful, even putting together IKEA furniture or doing a dump run. Any time I get with Jeff is a treat.

- Watching '90s action movies. I know every Sylvester Stallone movie by heart!

- Seeing a lighthouse.

- Exploring Canada, from coast to coast to coast.

- Petting any dog. Seeing a dog's head out a car window— you know it is going to be a good day if you see a dog riding in a car, living their best life!

- Making up "quests" when I visit other cities and countries, like exploring Graceland in Memphis while listening to Marc Cohn's "Walking in Memphis" at sunrise, or running up Masada in Israel listening to Journey's "Don't Stop Believin'." Seriously: pick a place and soundtrack and make your own adventure. Oh, the joy of being in a real moment and making a memory!

- Calling the saints by name, out loud, when you need their intercession. When Hunter was writing one of his grade nine exams, we may have said a prayer to Saint Jude (patron saint of impossible cases). When he was going into his grade ten exams, Hunter playfully said we did not need Saint Jude's help this semester! That was a good sign!

- Hugging the children after their bath or shower, when they are in their PJs and having a puppy pileup cuddle on the couch. Nothing compares to holding your babies even when they are now bigger than you!

- Seeing my family's faces for the first time after we have been apart. I ache to see them, and when I do, my heart finds rest.

- A clean kitchen in the morning and the sound of the coffee pot. Simple but joy-filled!

I hope you see here that your list should reflect you and your personal relationship with joy. Find your unique moments, things, and events that bring you joy, and make room for more of it all! The more *you*, the better!

Wonder and Awe

Another way some people report experiencing humour is through being inspired. The goal of humour is to lift the weight off your shoulders and soften your heart. Some people are not the laughing and playful type. And that is completely okay.

I was working with a leader of one of the largest banks in Canada, and we were discussing and reflecting on humour. They shared that they never really felt connected with their funny side, and this was the area of my theory they wanted to learn more about. We landed upon the idea that if the goal of the humour element of resiliency is to soften, then perhaps we could find this somewhere else. In the coaching session, they decided that the idea of wonder and awe could serve the same purpose.

So, if rolling around, playing, and laughing does not connect with you, perhaps you could explore the idea of wonder and awe. When was the last time something took your breath away, when time seemed to stand still, just for that moment, so your senses could try and take it all in? When do you feel awestruck or mesmerized by the wonder of our world?

Many of us are so busy with the constant ebb and flow of our daily lives that the idea of wonder and awe seems distant. Maybe you reserve this notion of truly looking at the world with wonder for when you are travelling or seeing something new. I invite you to think about how we can see the wonder in the everyday. I think that sometimes we gloss over the everyday because if we stopped and look closely at the world around, we wouldn't get anything done. If we marvelled at how our bodies actually worked or thought about even how our cars worked, we would become so overwhelmed with knowledge, complexity, and the sheer vastness of moving parts, we wouldn't be able to get anything done! Researcher Pamela Paresky, author of a *Year of Kindness*, explains that wonder and awe are extremely important in our everyday practices of wellness. She describes wonder as an act of intellectual humility. If we know everything, we cannot experience wonder. We need to adopt a humble outlook and be willing to learn.[5]

Awe is believed to be a sense of collective engagement and oneness to the world around us. It is how we can find our common threads and links to humanity. It is the tapestry of not only our lives, but also the lives of those who have gone before us. When we work with these definitions, it is easier to see why these practices are so important for our lives.

When I was younger, I came upon Viktor Frankl's 1946 book, *Man's Search for Meaning*. This classic will be in my top five books for life. Frankl writes about his experiences surviving the most horrific events as a prisoner in Auschwitz. He used those experiences to form what we now call logotherapy, the psychological practice of helping people find meaning in their lives, including in the suffering. Frankl argued that the ability to choose one's attitude was of paramount importance for survival: "Everything can be taken from a man but one thing; the last of the human freedoms—to choose one's attitude in any given set of circumstances."[6] He also wrote about the importance of being mindful about what we choose to focus upon. I still remember reading this passage for the first time, through tears and with a sense of absolute wonder. Frankl shared a conversation between two prisoners in the concentration camp:

> Standing outside we saw sinister clouds glowing in the west and the whole sky alive with clouds of ever-changing shapes and colours, from steel blue to blood red. The desolate grey mud huts provided a sharp contrast, while the puddles on the muddy ground reflected the glowing sky. Then, after minutes of moving silence, one prisoner said to another, "How beautiful the world could be!"[7]

We can use the principles of wonder and awe for fostering resiliency by choosing to view our lives from a higher plane. Taking that step back. Being willing to be humble. When we are in the valley, we sometimes forget the views of the mountain ranges. Even in the direst conditions, with great effort, we can choose where we set our gaze. A humble heart and a fierce mind will serve you well. Find wonder. Be in awe.

"Smile
and let go
it's just life
afterall
and you're
doing alright
just by
living."
ATTICUS

WHEN ALL ELSE FAILS, WHICH IT WILL, DON'T TAKE LIFE TOO SERIOUSLY

There's a well-known quote that goes something like this: "None of us are going to make it out of this life alive." We already know that our time on earth is limited, and our stories will end. We are all mortal. This is one of the most basic truths in life. Grief is a wicked beast. Pain is real. Suffering hurts. Anxiety is scary. And we never truly bounce back from loss or trauma—it becomes part of the fabric of our lives, and that is completely okay, even when it really does not feel like it. Despite the daily challenges, we can choose to see each day as an opportunity to learn new skills to help carry the load of life. My wish for you is that you stay open-hearted. Stay humble and curious enough to see the humour, joy, wonder, and awe that is still to be had while you are here. The same life that is hard is also wondrous and beautiful. It is inspiring. It is breathtaking. We are still here. Goodness is out there. Love will prevail. As Mr. Rogers said, when you see all the tragedy in the world, "look for the helpers. You will always find people who are helping."[8]

FINDING THE HUMOUR WHEREVER YOU ARE AND WHEREVER YOU GO

As a parent of three children, at any given moment my heart can be in four places at once: with me and with the three children wherever they happen to be. Recently, my heart was with me in San Diego and 4,281 kilometres away with Jaxson in Peterborough, Ontario. It was team-selection weekend for his representative basketball program—two days of testing and evaluation. By the end of Sunday, he would have a spot on the roster or he would be released.

I had already signed a contract to be in San Diego for the same weekend and could not change my speaking tour commitment. Of course, everything seems to fall on the same weekend! I felt torn and left for San Diego with a heavy heart. I shifted into professional speaker mode and was doing my best to focus on the task at hand. I had just checked into my hotel and was having a coffee at a beachfront café in Coronado, reviewing my presentation, when Jaxson called me.

"Mama, you need to come home now," he said. He explained that the first round of tryouts did not go well. Some other players really got into this head, and he never got to touch the ball and did not feel like the coaching staff even noticed him. This was a new team for Jaxson, and the players from the previous year's team were not making it easy for a new kid to make the cut. "Mama, I need you here," he said. "I cannot do this without you. Please come home now. I need you."

My heart ached and I tried my best to console him from afar. I tried everything I could possibly do and say to be his champion, but the truth was, it was not working. When I finally explained that under no circumstance could I even make it home if I flew out that night, I could hear his disappointment loud and clear. I had let him down. I simply could not fix this.

We ended the call, and I cried behind sunglasses at one of the most beautiful beaches in the world. After a thorough personal guilt trip, hosted by me, for me, I finally came up with a plan. I knew Jeff and Hunter could do this. Jeff would be able to give Jaxson some tips and strategies for reflecting, reframing, and resetting. Hunter could do the athlete-to-athlete talk. Hunter had navigated countless team-selection weekends. I rallied my troops back home for their help. Jeff and Hunter were on it.

I asked Hunter for one more special job. It went something like this. En route to the team selection the next day, Hunter gave Jaxson a pre-tryout speech. He would hit on the key ideas about choosing to be brave and the importance of being willing to take the risk. Hunter took excerpts from the "Man in the Arena" speech by Theodore Roosevelt (he and I both love that one). He referenced Rocky, David Goggins, and every basketball hero he could think of. After the speech, Hunter followed my next steps to a T. I instructed Hunter to give Jaxson his headphones, play a particular song for him, and tell Jaxson the song was from me. Now, before I tell you what song I wanted Hunter to play for Jaxson, please be mindful that desperate times call for desperate measures. I asked Hunter to play a terribly-not-age-appropriate rap song by the artist Ludacris. Please note: I am not endorsing this type of song for kids. The gist is that we found Jax a hype song! I knew it would it work for Jaxson in this moment.

Hunter told Jaxson, "Mama is sending you this song. She says to sharpen your elbows, get out there, and move those players out of your head and out of your way. This is your court: defend it, own it. Leave nothing but everything you've got on that hardwood. Mama says make them move and get this done."

Hunter said Jaxson totally changed in that moment. Instead of being nervous and timid, Jaxson laughed and took the court with an intensity and urgency to prove to the coaching staff that he deserved to be noticed. Jaxson was fuelled by courage and fearlessness and had a totally inappropriate anthem in his mind that his mama sent him, with love, from

San Diego. My badass little baller-thug was not going to let fear and a few other players get in the way of his goal.

Moments into the tryout, a few parents, who knew I was travelling with work, texted me to say that Jaxson was demolishing the tryout. Hunter texted me, too, to tell me that Jaxson was "breaking ankles out there" (a basketball term for when the opponent makes the other players lose their balance and fall down). Jaxson was on fire. The next text message was from Jeff: "He is smiling and having fun out there—problem solved." Jaxson called me after the tryout. "Thanks, Mama... I got it done. Now you go get it done in San Diego. See you tomorrow!"

My intention in this chapter was to provide an overview of how humour relates to my theory of resiliency and how you can start exploring practices that promote this in your own life. In times of stress, change, challenge, and uncertainty, humour is often the first thing to go, but interestingly, it is in those tense times when we need it the most. Humour allows us to have momentary relief and a chance to believe that we will be okay again. This is a gentle invitation to soften your heart and the creases on your forehead! As previously mentioned, the major conclusion from researchers is that humour has a broad range of effects on perceptions, attitudes, judgements, and emotions, which in turn directly and indirectly support our physical and psychological states. This is significant. I am thankful that this last variable, the one that was so tricky to name, has its own chapter and holds an important role within the model alongside the other four variables. Upon reflection, I think it is funny that this element brings me the most merriment every chance I see it within the people I am so honoured to work with!

"The person who has
a sense of humor is not
just more relaxed in
the face of a potentially
stressful situation,
but is more flexible in
his approach."

JOHN MORREALL

THE BIG IDEAS OF PART III

In Part III, I introduced the five variables that make up the new model of everyday resiliency. This model shows how a baseline for resiliency is generated. It captures how a person's ability to navigate stress, challenge, change, uncertainty, and all the things that we must carry in life derives energy and focus from the five traits. Together, these pillars form our baseline for resiliency that we carry into every new experience.

Resiliency is not something you have or do not have. It is our self-efficacy, our belief that we can navigate the hard parts of our lives. I believe that what it means to be resilient comes from the foundation of deep belonging, the first variable of the model. We need to have roots. We need to know that we matter and to see ourselves as part of something bigger. Our sense of belonging is deeply entwined with our identity and connects our lives to those of our ancestors. It is imperative that we recognize that we are here, we matter, and we carry on the legacy of those who have walked before us.

The second variable is perspective, the capacity to have flexible and nimble thinking. Often, we see people hold brittle thinking or ideas that allow little room for new ideas or growth. Our capacity to be flexible and bend serves us well in times of change and uncertainty. Those who successfully navigate challenging times know how to adjust their sails.

The third variable is acceptance. The capacity to learn and grow. Life has a tendency to prune and shape us, much as Mother Earth does to all of nature. When we resist and push against life, we run the risk of getting stuck. I see people who for decades have been stuck in an event that they do not understand. They constantly ruminate on why things happened, and often, there is no answer. Acceptance does not mean that we have to like what has happened in our lives, but rather that we are willing to acknowledge it. We need to start asking different questions, like, "Is how I am currently thinking about this working or not working? Is this serving me or holding me back?" It is also helpful to remember that we do not have to accept all of it. We just have to accept the exact moment we are in right now. Fretting about tomorrow or wondering how you will ever possibly get over something does not serve you. Accept the moment. You will soon see you are well equipped to do just that.

The fourth variable is hope and being hopeful. One of the most profound truths I have come upon in my work is the idea that hope is a choice. It is something we find within ourselves and then choose to put out in the world.

Finally, I present the variable of humour in all its messiness! I posit the idea that humour, joy, awe and wonder, and light-heartedness can serve as a buffer in times of trial and help us both physically and psychologically.

I want to acknowledge that there is a component of social equity in resiliency as well. Some people are better positioned than others in their lives to be able to enact these traits. However, I do see the five pillars of resiliency as being intrinsically driven. I have played with children in orphanages in developing countries who have never experienced privilege and resources yet still hold a deep sense of belonging. I have coached top-level executives who have an abundance of privilege and resources yet can hold perspective of what it was like to work in the mailroom when they first started. I have shared time with emergency room doctors who after a community mass-shooting tragedy that was plastered across the country's headline news, practiced acceptance. They were mindfully aware of what was within their control and what was not. (I like to call these things our "controllables.")

These doctors grieved while persisting. Young girls in a refugee camp shared with me their hope for their future despite
their families having lived in refugee camps for three generations. They know they will be the ones who rise. They choose
to live a hope-filled life. And lastly, I have seen police officers
treated brutally by the very people they are sworn to protect
and still maintain a smile on their faces while de-escalating
a situation with humour, tact, and poise. Conversely, I know
that some police officers treat people they are sworn to protect in a brutal manner. This deeply hurts the hearts of good
officers as well as communities. It is not okay. Yet they and
the communities persist.

The capacity for resiliency is universal. The human spirit
is limitless and knows no boundaries.

Next, in Part IV, I will present the paths to everyday resiliency. The reality is that being resilient is a process and
practice. Life is relentless, and it will always provide ample
opportunities for us to practice being resilient. There is a
quote often attributed to Mother Teresa: "I know God will
not give me anything I can't handle." Well, clearly, God thinks
we are a bunch of badass warriors, because this thing called
life is hard! But thankfully we are all well equipped.

PART IV

— THE —

PATHS

"

It is never too late to change
your course. And it is not wrong to
hope someone else does, either.
Our past comes with us on our chosen
paths as wisdom, and our supporters
become the knowledge holders for
how far we have come.

"

CHAPTER 11

THE RESILIENCY TRAJECTORY MODEL

M Y INTENTION NOW is to share with you what resiliency looks like in action. I want to show you how thinking about resiliency on a trajectory of experience equips us to navigate the hard stuff. I want to help you create a reunion between your life circumstances and your head and heart that fits within the life you want to be living. The four paths I will describe are a lot like phases. I call them "paths" because, to me, that represents that this is a journey, a progression. These paths represent starting points for doing this "heart" work of resiliency after an adverse event. Think of them as gentle invitations, informed by research, that other people have accepted and that served them well. Before we talk more specifically about these paths, however, let us frame resiliency on a continuum so we can shift theory into practice.

THE RESILIENCY TRAJECTORY MODEL

Having worked with people for over two decades in a variety of settings such as hospitals; clinics; prisons; elementary, college, and university classrooms; and large business, corporate, and health care organizations; and with first responders, military personnel, and high-performance athletes, I have come to an understanding of how people lean into different parts of life to form a baseline. You can think of it as having resiliency reservoirs of internal and external variables that you lean or dig into to help you find the motivation, commitment, and strength to keep going. What do people dig into when life gets hard or they face a challenge? A person's belief that they can get through a difficult experience or seasons becomes their self-efficacy. Now I want to show you how this all comes together in an application.

My work here is inspired by and grounded in a framework developed by educational giants Jerry Patterson, from the University of Alabama, and Paul Kelleher, from Trinity University, in their book, *Resilient School Leaders*.[1] The diagram below is a modified version of a chart that originally appeared as a figure in the book. My modifications reflect what I have seen in my work and extend the model's applicability beyond only educational leaders.

FIGURE 1: **Dr. RHD's Resiliency Trajectory Model**

The diagram on the left represents how resiliency unfolds. First, we have our baseline resiliency, which is formed by the five core competencies (belonging, perspective, acceptance, hope, and humour). These five areas in turn form a person's self-efficacy, or belief that they can do hard things. Next, the adverse event happens. The event can be anything that creates the moment everything stands still, when we are thrust into the present. We look life in the eye and are absolutely attuned in that moment. We are omnipresent in our own life. The event could be an injury—say, an athlete suddenly blowing out their knee while playing a sport. They probably were not thinking about the knee or giving it all of their focus and attention until the injury occurred. Or maybe you are in a traffic accident. Driving, you are not really thinking about your car, until it is suddenly crumpled, and now it is top of mind. Or you get a phone call or message that your medical report is not good. Or a knock on the door—when you open it, your life will never be the same again. The adverse event is that moment that screams at you that there is a plot twist or a full-on life trauma taking centre stage right now, whether temporarily or permanently. When we are in that moment, we start progressing through four distinct phases of resiliency.

Decline Phase

When adversity strikes, as it inevitably will, we start the journey of navigating through four phases. Every event that rocks us will leave an initial mark. This is normal regardless of one's resiliency prior to the event. If you are not even slightly impacted by the adverse event, it does not require you to practice resiliency. You need to be knocked down to get back up or bounce back. Again, if there is no decline, it is not an event

"It is when I struggle
that I strengthen.
It is when challenged
to my core that I learn
the depth of who I am."

STEVE MARABOLI

requiring resiliency. The degree of the decline is relative to your pre-adversity self-efficacy score. Even the most resilient people take some time and make space to regroup, refocus, readjust, and land on what just happened. I see people put such pressure on themselves to bounce back immediately after a setback. You need to give yourself permission to land first, evaluate the damage, observe the collateral impacts, and then decide. You can stay here for as long as it takes. Getting through difficulties is not a race. People who bounce back without acknowledging and recognizing the impact usually have to come back and do that work later. And coming back to it later is much, much harder. That is why I am so mindful of the immediate next steps after experiencing a crisis or major setback. What we do during the decline phase matters to our recovery. When you skip the pain, you skip your lessons. Knowledge will not keep the pain away. The only way is to go through it, moment by moment, feeling by feeling, with an open heart and mind.

Adapt Phase

This is the phase when we adjust, shift, prioritize, and practice our flexibility. When I am working with people here, I often call this the need for our flexible thinking, or the cognitive nimbleness period. In my core competencies model, this is the perspective element. In many self-help books, it is referred to as establishing the "new normal." I recall someone telling me that I needed to embrace my new normal. I recoiled at this terminology. I did not want a new normal. I rejected this language wholeheartedly. But what did eventually resonate with me was the idea of having to do a "course correction." You were on your journey, the storm hit, now you must adjust your sails and recalibrate your course. My heart could get on board with this line of thinking. Storms happen. That is part of nature. Nature adapts.

Reclaim Phase

This phase is where I see people taking back their stories. After adapting, we can reclaim our lives. Through self-compassion, wisdom, and honouring our soul we can bravely make room for the adversity to be *part* of our story—it does not *define* our story. We are not our mistakes, accidents, or pain. They are events, not characteristics. Unfortunately, many do not get to this phase—they are completely and utterly stuck in the adverse event. As I explained in chapter 8 on acceptance, people get stuck in the "why is this happening to me?" loop and never escape. Horrible things happen. Life is not fair. Following every rule will not guarantee a life without hurt, disappointment, or injustice. At one point or another, we will get knocked down by life. That is a guarantee. It is what we do with those million shattered pieces that matters. So the reclaim phase is when we pick up those million pieces, hurt by hurt, and create a new masterpiece, a mosaic that represents a truly lived and a boldly experienced life.

Rise Phase

This is when we are far enough on the other side of the adversity that we can rise. This phase is not just getting back up; it is truly rising. It is a rebirth, a resurrection, and a reunion with our life. At this point, while we have been truly impacted by the adversity, we have still transformed into wiser and more connected humans. This is where empathy and compassion prevail, not bitterness and judgement. As we progress through each of these phases, we truly learn who we are and what we are capable of. Each event becomes evidence of our strength, fortitude, and openness to learning and growing. Every lived experience that goes through these phases is ultimately transforming us. It holds true the idea that you cannot change what has happened, but you can decide what you do next, and that matters.

FIGURE 2: **Resiliency Trajectory Model Sample**

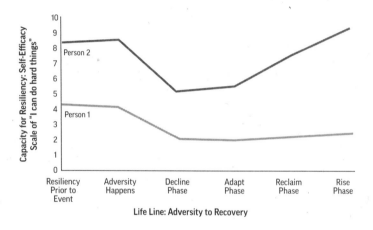

In Figure 1 above, I presented the Resiliency Trajectory Model. Figure 2 is an example of two people working through the model. The Y axis is the Capacity for Resiliency/Self-Efficacy Score, or the "I can do hard things scale" (from 0 = "I can't" to 10 = "I can"). The X axis is our life in time over a series of phases. As we progress through life, we have a relatively set score of self-efficacy regarding our capacity for resiliency. In this case, self-efficacy is our belief that we can do hard things. This notion is deeply impacted by our sense of belonging and our capacity for being accepting and hopeful. As evident in Figure 1, the baseline score of resilient efficacy will determine the pitch of the decline phase. In Figure 2, Person 1 is moving forward through time but is not making much progress through the phases. Person 2 is moving forward and is making gains in each phase. The trajectory for Person 2 suggests that they will not only bounce back but be stronger for it. Person 1 appears to be stuck. It may take more time for them to progress, or they may consciously or unconsciously decide to stay stuck, living a life defined by the adverse event.

Now, let's take a closer look at these phases as paths. To help illustrate the idea of pathways, it interesting to use a literary approach. I love how we can map Joseph Campbell's hero's journey archetype onto this work.[2] Campbell's hero's journey, detailed in his 1949 book, *The Hero with a Thousand Faces*, encompasses the idea that every great story has a pattern. It is awesome to think that Jesus Christ, Luke Skywalker, William Wallace, Joan of Arc, Jane Eyre, and even Anne of Green Gables can fit along similar arcs. The concept holds the idea that each person goes through a series of experiences that make them a hero. There are many competing views on how many paths are part of the hero's journey, but the simplified version looks like this: There is a call to adventure; you enter the unknown; you meet challenges and temptations; you have to slay dragons; and then there is a proverbial death and rebirth.

To examine this model in relation to resiliency, the call to adventure is more of an adverse experience that triggers the action and subsequent stages. As we choose how we progress through this experience that requires personal resiliency,

"You can't go back
and change the beginning,
but you can start where you
are and change the ending."

C. S. LEWIS

we will enter the unknown. Despite all we know about psychology, science, and the human condition, how each person experiences their journey is unique. Sure, there are similarities, patterns, and general ideas, but what everything feels like is personalized. Every life experience informs what our pain, loss, challenge, and grief will feel like. Like in the hero's journey, as we navigate the unknown, we will come upon challenges and even temptations. For example, after an injury we will feel pain, and we may even be tempted to give up. We decide getting better is not worth the fight. Or perhaps we face a challenge that in our mind is insurmountable, and we are tempted to surrender what matters most to us.

I remember supporting a single mother who, after two gruelling years in a vicious custody battle that involved her son with a disability, she hit a point where she could not keep going. The son's father was a prestigious man with more resources. He used the child against her. She knew she was in the right, but she had run out of financial resources and her emotional health was so depleted, she entertained the idea of just walking away. She confided in me that this thought scared her, and she was ashamed to say it out loud. I remember squeezing her hand so hard and imploring her to rest before she quit. If you must walk away, that is your choice, but first catch your breath, take the rest you need, and recharge.

We must slay our dragons to become better versions of ourselves. Again, everyone's dragon is going to look different. In my recovery as a teenager with mental health challenges, one of the dragons I slayed was self-harm. I made the personal oath to never use self-harm as a means of communication again. I committed to "telling people, not showing people" my pain. This promise I made to myself, which I am honoured to have kept and continue to keep, took self-harm off the table for me as a form of communication. I took that dragon down.

Sometimes the dragons are external, and we overcome them through many different means—sometimes we leave, or fight, or distance, or even ignore or surrender. The idea is that the dragon no longer has a hold on us. We refuse to be victims. Other times, those dragons are internal, and we must address them with as much commitment, intention, and fortitude as we give the external threats. Both have the same goal: get past this so we can be better versions of ourselves.

Through the act of conquering or healing our dragons, there is death and rebirth. Now, we have come full circle. We return as a changed person who has a mighty tale, which we can choose to share or tuck away. Some of our greatest battles are fought with no one bearing witness but us. And that is okay. Share or protect your story. That is your choice.

This idea of resiliency overlaid on the hero's journey is an amazing tool for growth and recovery. I have seen first-hand how viewing one's life or a difficult experience through the hero's journey lens can been transformative for people. This is one of my favourite coaching tools to support writing our personal narratives. Now, let us return to my Resiliency Trajectory Model, and I will share more about each one of the phases.

66

Not every storm that comes
into your life is meant to take
you down. Perhaps that storm is
coming to clear a path that you
could never have found otherwise.

99

CHAPTER 12

THE FOUR PHASES

THE DECLINE PHASE

When the adverse event happens, we are often left completely and totally helpless. Sometimes we do not see it coming, and other times, we knew this day would come. Each event can start a cascade of huge emotions, racing thoughts, unspeakable physical pain. For some people, nothing comes. Absolute nothingness. Our body protects us by going into shock. There are eight symptoms of psychological trauma:

1 Shock, denial, or disbelief
2 Confusion, difficulty concentrating
3 Anger, irritability, mood swings
4 Anxiety and fear
5 Guilt, shame, self-blame
6 Withdrawing from others
7 Feeling sad or hopeless
8 Feeling disconnected or numb[1]

It is imperative that we remember that these responses are normal reactions to abnormal events. I try to remind people to minimize the blast radius and additional harm. In the moment, we need to focus solely on personal safety and security. Think decision to decision, not about later. Just be here now.

Ken Druck writes about how to manage when coping with a major life event or tragedy and makes a series of recommendations.[2] I added guide words to help serve as prompts.

1 Pace yourself: the journey ahead will be long. *One breath at a time.*

2 Take breaks and come up for air: shut it down when you need to. *Stop and pause.*

3 Be patient with yourself: there is no right way to feel. *Just be.*

4 Forgive yourself: you cannot control what happened. *Forgive and surrender.*

5 Prioritize self-care: do the basics. *Just do the next right thing for me.*

6 Release all self-criticism: be kind to yourself. *Use gentle words.*

7 Express emotions: feel it as you can. *Name it and let it pass.*

8 Surround yourself with support: you are not alone. *I have roots.*

9 Keep your faith: trust. *There is a season for everything.*

10 Do not give yourself a timeline: Just the next right decision. *I am here.*

"You were unsure which pain is worse—the shock of what happened or the ache for what never will."

SIMON VAN BOOY

I believe people are their own experts. You know yourself better than anyone else on this planet! You will know when you are ready to enter the adapt phase. You do not have to move there all at once. It is with slow and cautious steps that we tentatively move forward.

Alissa, the Teacher

I know as a professor we are not supposed to have favourite students, but sometimes a student comes into your classroom and changes your life. For me, this student was Alissa. She was in my second-year psychology course, and she was such a bright light. She was eager, motivated, hardworking, and a delightful student to get to know. Alissa was so on her way to being the most epic elementary school teacher you could ever hope your child would have. I was so impressed by her approach and philosophy as a future educator that after our course ended, my husband and I hired her as a tutor for our children. I wanted them to see Alissa's love of learning. She was so curious and inspiring. She made me want to be in grade school again to see it through her eyes.

Alissa instantly became part of our family. Her future was on-course and she would soar. It was just so obvious that she was going to be an amazing educator, on top of being just such a joyful person.

However, as we all know, sometimes life blindsides you. In Alissa's case, it was on a perfect July afternoon when she was on her way to a friend's cottage. She was a passenger in a head-on collision that changed her life forever. What Alissa survived is nothing less than miraculous. The countless surgeries and months and months in the hospital and rehab were a testament to her courage and strength. It is almost inconceivable that a body could go through all that. Yet despite all that pain, hurt, and loss, Alissa's spirit and character never changed. The catastrophic brain injury did not dim her light. Alissa's decline phase lasted years. She grieved the life she never got to live. But she was alive. Her little frame carried inexplicable pain with grace and poise.

Over time, she recommitted to building what life she could after the accident. Alissa has walked a path I believe many people could not have. Her physical recovery was astonishing, but the forgiveness and tenderness she carries in all that she does is like nothing I have ever seen before. She is as eager, motivated, hardworking, and enthusiastic as before her accident, but now she is also the mightiest and kindest five-foot woman I have ever met. Seeing her in the ICU after her accident and the scars left behind remind me that she had a decline phase. For Alissa, her previous idea of her life had to completely fall apart before she could rebuild. One of the bravest things I have ever witnessed was Alissa letting go of how she thought her life would be. And then, after she learned to walk again, she walked right into her future with an open heart. Alissa is our chosen family. She is the big sister and auntie to the children, and the little sister I never knew I needed. We have the honour of knowing not only her but some of her family too. Her dad, Tom, her mom, Kim, and her dear grandfather, Ben, are extraordinary people who walked beside Alissa every day of her recovery. I think Tom's love of the University of Notre Dame's Fighting Irish helped shape Alissa's way of being in this world. Notre Dame's motto is *Vita, Dulcedo, Spes*: Life, Sweetness, Hope. That sums up Alissa.

Today, Alissa is the master teacher I believed she would be all those years ago when our paths first crossed. Although the curriculum she teaches now is not in elementary schools as a

educator, she teaches all of us, who know her, by her example.
Despite all the odds, Alissa graduated university. She demonstrates what it means to be mightier than your pain and braver
than your fears. Alissa will tell you I am one of her favourite
teachers, but truth be told, she is one of mine.

THE ADAPT PHASE

The adapt phase is when we start learning. In the event of
adversity, we are thrust into seeing the world differently.
We absolutely do not have to like what is happening, and
we do not have to see the silver lining. There may be nothing good that comes from an adverse experience, and that is
completely and totally okay. This phase is not about finding
meaning; it is about discovering what we need to do to keep
our heads above the water. In the decline phase it feels like
we may have forgotten how to swim, but in the adapt phase
we realize that we need to find a way to keep moving our arms
and legs. We learn how to keep going.

The adapt phase happens whether we like it or not. The
aim of this phase is adjusting. It is learning the new skills we
need to stay afloat in light of what we are going through. It
is learning to take one moment at a time and be. Even while
we are in the decline phase, we are already treading in the
adapt phase. We essentially have to immediately start shifting, adjusting, and recalibrating our lives after the event. It is
common, if the event is major, for this moment to become the
flagstone that marks a before and an after within our life story.

This was my case and that of many people I have worked
with. Our lives become divided. For me, my dividing line is my
mom's passing. It marks my life with her and my life without her.

"As the legend goes, when the Phoenix resurrects from the flames, she is even more beautiful than before."

DANIELLE LAPORTE

My Mom

I remember driving to the lake house the day after I lost my mother and being completely perplexed that the rest of the world was going on as usual. Our planet was still spinning. Traffic lights still changed. News still happened. The radio played. My world disintegrated and then evaporated in a mere instant. Lesley was here and then Lesley was not here. I had a mother and then my mother was dead. My mother did not deserve to die like she did. My mother's time here was not up. I still needed her.

My mother, Lesley, was kind, loving, devoted, faith-filled, generous, accepting, forgiving, and self-sacrificing. She was clever, funny, hard-working, patient, feisty, and tender. Lesley was a gifted listener. Her attention was like a light she would shine on everyone she spoke to. People loved talking with her. Her quiet confidence in life and her faith comforted both the young and old. She was a hands-on, minds-on, hearts-on, full-on "grammie" to her grandchildren. And those grandchildren adored her. My mom was also brave. She was a protector.

During the storm of my adolescence, a room full of psychologists told my mom, in front of me, that she was enabling me, and I was a lost cause. "You need to remove her from your home," they said. "She won't survive to see her eighteenth birthday. She needs to learn the consequences of her behaviour. You need to start distancing yourself from her now." My mom looked those psychologists in the eye and in a quiet but committed and strong voice said, "Thank you for your opinion, but no. I will never give up on my daughter. She will get through this. We will get through this." And then she reached for my hand, and we walked out.

My mom's conviction, her faith, her belief in me, and her unconditional love is how and why I started to recover. At first, I was getting better for her, and then I started getting better for me. My mother promised me that one day I would meet my children. That I would have a future. That I would find my path. She said that my struggle would one day help others. "This isn't happening to you in vain, Robyne," she told me. "Your story will allow you to be of service to others. You getting better will be an example—that it is never too late, or a teenager is never too far gone, to change the course of their life. I will love you hard through all of this. You are already on your way, little one," she said.

If a mother's love could prevent harm, my mother's love would have shielded me from every pain in this world. What a mother's love can do is foster hope. It can protect that little light in our soul. She stood up for me, and boldly said no to the world, when the world said my fight was over. I am Lesley's daughter.

Oh, how I hated every single second of life without my mom when she passed. Every second added to the time that we were apart. While I was in the decline phase, the notion of adapting was excruciating and totally not plausible. I was well prepared and willing to live in the darkness of grief and anger. My adolescence had taught me how to shut down and armour up. I would never bounce back from this. If I were to recover, it would be as though I was dishonouring her or the scope of my loss. I would not adjust. As I shared earlier in the book, I had survived many trials, but this was the one thing I said I couldn't do. I couldn't raise my children without my mom. I dug in my heels and gave the world a big "fuck you." My rebellious heart was ready to release a lifetime of hurt, anger, and meanness. No more benevolent Robyne. I felt rage that had been bottled up since those first episodes of bullying in senior kindergarten, and I was ready to unleash hell. I did not even care who I took out in the process.

Oh, but wait: I was on carpool duty. I had to get the children to school. And then I had to make dinner. And then I had to do laundry. And then I had to go to basketball. And then I had to tuck the children into their beds and read them stories. And then I had to walk the dog. My grief in the form of a mental collapse and behavioural explosion would have to wait. I decided after my mom's funeral that I would have to hold off on losing my mind for a while. I had to keep going, moment by moment, despite all the pain and fear, because she would have wanted her grandbabies to have dinner. That is what I told myself. The only thing that kept me going was the idea that my mom would have expected me to, and she had high expectations about how to love your kids.

Shortly after the initial shock of losing her, I realized that I was already adjusting. My mom had been preparing me my whole life for the time we would be apart. She had taught me how to be a mother who loves her children more than evolution requires us to. She taught me our family values. My parents created a loving home that showed me the importance of hard work, kindness, and doing what is right. My mom even picked out the right husband for her and the best dad for me. My parents were married for nearly forty years. My dad was exactly who I needed. She equipped him too. He and I would grow closer than I ever could have imagined. He would shine as a grandfather who would shepherd in the next clan of Hanleys. The grandchildren would be okay. I would be okay. We would all be okay. We were well equipped. She made sure of it. My mom taught me I can do hard things.

I started cataloguing every one of my favourite parts of my mom in my brain and backed it up in my heart. I created a mental vault to hold all the parts of her I could. I was architecting a way to solidify her existence in my soul. My mom would not be a memory. My mom permeates every aspect of my life and that of her grandchildren's.

Adjusting seems counterintuitive at first, but it actually becomes part of every next step we take after adversity. Life keeps happening, and every step we take is an act of adjusting. The first place I go to when I need to adapt is nature. It is hard to adjust to the idea that the world will keep going. The traffic lights, world events, and society continue regardless of our pain. Society shows no empathy for our losses. If society knew the pain of losing a mother, they would not bombard the airwaves with Mother's Day advertisements. If society knew the ache of your children not having their grandmother, they would not plaster signs of grandmothers with their grandchildren everywhere, as if everyone should have this. If people knew how crippling the hurt is that you can never pick up a phone and call your mother or hear her voice, people would not complain that their mom called again! If people knew what it felt like to never be held by your mother again, they would not complain about having to drive to see her. But thank God, we have nature. Nature is real. Nature is big. Nature is our first home. Nature also shows compassion and mercy for our pain. The seasons are living testaments to the power of loss, change, adjusting, and adapting. Nature bows down to our pain with such gentleness if we look for it. The seasons are in a constant dance of shifting, ebbing, and flowing, always making room for what is and what is next. There is a season for everything.

"I am not what
happened to me.
I am what I choose
to become."

CARL JUNG

THE RECLAIM PHASE

To help unpack the reclaim phase, I turn to the brilliant autoethnography written by then-graduate student Natalie St-Denis. I have never met her, but when I came upon her work, I was inspired. St-Denis writes about her experience reclaiming her Indigenous identity. She writes poetically about how her reclaiming journey went through a series of phases: Wake, Exploring, Indigenizing, Reclaiming, Belonging, and Emerging Warrior.[3] This description of coming upon who she really is captures the essence of the reclaim phase for me. I thank St-Denis for writing so bravely.

First, we must awaken to what we can learn from the difficult experiences; then, we must explore. Like a detective, we must seek out answers to big questions. Then we can reclaim what we need. We can internalize the learning and the growth, what we will carry forward. Lastly, we find and develop the capacity to coexist with our past and future so as to become warriors who can do the hard things in life. This sums up the reclaim phase. We braid our life story back together.

It can be hard to separate who we actually are and what we have been told about ourselves. Society sets out norms and rules; families raise their children under these rules. I reflect on how different my life would have been if I hadn't grown up thinking that as a woman, I was supposed to finish school, get married, buy a house, and have two children by the time I was twenty-five. I do not remember anyone explicitly telling me that, but for some reason I picked up this messaging at a young age. I believe my mom actually tried to teach me the opposite, but I didn't listen. I listened to teenage dramas, movies, stories, and other forms of media. Instead of thinking about my future as an independent and contributing member of society and a global citizen, I believed that I had to be married first and foremost. Even the creation story I was taught as a child sent this message: Eve was made to serve Adam. There really is not much of an Eve story outside of Adam. There is a long list of beliefs that we have been taught that can hold us back, and often, we follow these beliefs unaware for a very long time until a crisis happens. It is usually only after a major event that we start re-evaluating, reflecting, and repairing. When we have no choice then but to look life in the eye.

The reclaim phase invites us to challenge what we know and decide how we want to proceed. If we view the adverse event as a crisis and a crisis is defined as a turning point, we have the opportunity to do three things: persist, pivot, or punt. We can persist and keep working toward what we want to achieve. We can pivot from our original idea and try a new approach. Or we can punt it away. We can decide that it no longer serves us, so we move on. The idea here is that we ultimately decide what we are going to do next. We take back our power from adversity.

The reclaim phase is both terrifying and wildly exciting. It is when we get to check in with ourselves, to think about how we truly feel about certain areas of our life. It is the phase in which we write the next part of our story with intention, purpose, and determination. It is when we pause long enough at the edge of the blast radius of the adverse event and take a step on the undamaged ground. We can still see the wreckage behind us, but we also can see new ground, calling to us. It is a gentle invitation to reconnect with our authentic self. It welcomes a reunion between who we were before and who we are becoming after the adverse event.

I also see this phase as the opportunity to let go of the "disease to please." Many of us struggle with the pressure to please others, or worry about what others will think of us. It feels selfish to look after ourselves first, but it is actually the opposite. Holding back your authentic self is mistreating and neglecting your gifts, talents, and essence. The world needs the real you.

People often ask two questions in this regard: "Who am I?" and "How do I know if this is my authentic self?" My best answer: trial and error. I also like this guiding principle: Make what matters most, matter most. I declared this when I blew out my fortieth-birthday candles—it was my prayer to myself, my family, and the world. I would reset my priorities from then on. Hate, doubters, "why" questions, stigma, negativity, gaslighters all be damned. You may pass through my day, but you will no longer be offered free room and board in my head and heart.

To get you started thinking about a reclaiming reunion, here is a little activity developed by Karen Benke to help promote this line of thinking.[4]

What matters most to you?

- My hands reach for...
- My feet run toward...
- My eyes search for...
- My soul wonders if...
- If you open the trapdoor of my heart, you'll find...

You can also ask yourself these questions (these are some of my favourites to ask someone in a coaching session to reflect on):

- What are my priorities?
- Where am I putting my time and energy? Does this align with what matters most to me?

- What will I regret not doing?
- What would my seven-year-old self be most proud of me for? How can I make her proud?
- What am I willing to do for the people I love?
- What am I willing to do for me that no one else can do?
- How do I want to be remembered?
- What will be my legacy?

The paramount idea in the reclaim phase is that your journey belongs to you now. Where you go and what you do next is totally and completely within your control. Just do the next right thing for you. And if you happen to not do the next right thing, try not to do two things in a row that don't serve you!

Another way to support your work in the reclaim phase could be to establish personal guideposts to ensure you are connecting and honouring your true self. Leadership development consultant Carley Hauck offers eight ways to be true to yourself:

1 Maintain alignment between what you feel and need and what you say and do.

2 Make values-based choices while considering intuition, research, and the bigger picture.

3 Do something each day that reflects your deepest needs, wishes, and values.

4 Speak up for yourself and ask for what you want.

5 Don't put up with abuse of any kind.

6 Give up designing your behavior by the desire to be liked (be imperfectly perfect and yourself!).

7 State and maintain your boundaries, especially about the level of energy you can handle being around or taking in.

8 Offer your fear loving-kindness and compassion.[5]

THE RISE PHASE

I do not believe that time heals. I believe that time allows for us to make space so our grief, pain, hurt, and setbacks can coexist with our life as we know it today. The rise phase is when we strike that balance. This is when we enact our deepest core values and choose to live them. Core values are extremely important to living our most resilient life; they serve as a compass for the direction in which we want to go. They highlight what we stand for while representing our uniqueness. These values will dictate our thoughts and behaviours. I think of them as your essence. They are your soul's wishes enacted in your daily life. Your values will lead you to the life you want to live through personal alignment. They reflect how you want to show up and ultimately how you will be and who you will become. Bill Watterson writes, "Creating a life that reflects your values and satisfies your soul is a rare achievement."[6] I believe that it is rare, but totally possible.

After an adverse event, we decline, then adapt, then reclaim, and then rise with our values intact or slightly modified or strengthened. Our values will naturally ebb and flow as we age, grow, learn, and experience setbacks, but there will be a consistency that likely will prevail. The aim of rising is to be aware of your values and how events reinforce how you choose to live your life. After the loss of my mom, I was temporarily pulled into a negative loop that made me want to abandon all my values and lessons I had been taught in life. Living a values-based life did not prevent bad things from happening. We may not be able to make meaning of our past. The answers to "why" questions will always be elusive. But we do get to choose how we want to live and be, and rise from the adversity. The greatest gift I can give to my mom now is to live a values-based life and teach those values to her grandchildren. So, when we see one another again, I can share with her stories that I would be proud to tell her and show her how her legacy continued. My mom's love mattered.

Having your values front of mind makes life easier to navigate. It is easier to make decisions when you use your values as a guide. It is in the discipline of living a values-based life that we can find our freedom—we do not have to overthink everything and wonder what others will say. We decide based on our values. We just know.

Be sure that your values are truly yours and not idealized versions of what you think you should value. Brené Brown shares her values list in her book *Dare to Lead: Brave Work. Tough Conversations. Whole Hearts.* Like other authors on this subject, including James Clear, author of *Atomic Habits*,[7] Brown suggests selecting three core values, and no more than five. This is the time to revisit your values that you explored in chapter 6. Instead of thinking about them as value areas, cull your list to your top three (or five) value words. These words form your personal motto. I have included a few here as an example of how to form your value word sets.

- Honesty, Authenticity, Kindness
- Patience, Compassion, Belief
- Family, Freedom, Health
- Justice, Openness, Perseverance

- Respect, Service, Success
- Uniqueness, Usefulness, Vision
- Vulnerability, Well-Being, Wholeheartedness

What are your guiding values? What would your set look like? Once you have your short list, pause. Reflect on whether these are your true values or values you think you should have. You may have to revisit your list a few times. There is no judgement. Think of this exercise as you giving your soul the language that we speak on earth. There are no rights or wrongs here. Your soul does not need to abide by earthly rules!

The rise phase is when we come to the other side of our adverse experience, transformed. We can never go back to what we were before the event—that way of being is no longer possible. And that is okay. I think it is important to note here, too, that whatever adversity we are recovering from could have been our own doing. That is okay too. Regardless of how it happened or who is responsible, the aim is forward motion. Sitting with blame, guilt, shame, and regret will not serve anyone. Sometimes the greatest act of rising is forgiving yourself. You have risen from your yesterday and bravely accept today. It is not what you did or were that matters, it is how you show up today in this very moment. The present moment is all we have.

Andrew Comes Back

What can happen if we rise from our past and become present? Let me tell you about one of my other favourite students, Andrew. He was in several of my psychology courses, and unlike Alissa, who was always keen and never missed a class, Andrew sat near the back and seemed distracted.

After one class, he stopped me as we were leaving and told me he was done. Even though he had only a few credits left to graduate with his degree, he could not find the drive to continue. He was physically, mentally, and emotionally spent. Although he had been successful up to that point in his university courses, he had hit a wall. Unlike many of his classmates, Andrew was working full time and volunteering as well as attending school full time. He was tired. He didn't feel like he could finish the semester. He confided in me that he really did not feel like university was for him.

I have spent a lot of time talking with students about this! Many students do not feel as though they fit into the academy. In my opinion, it is because university is not really designed for anyone outside of the box. It is a system that works on the principle of replicating. Great students usually become professors who love to teach great students like them.[8]

Now, this is not always the case. I know so many wonderful professors who care deeply about supporting their students regardless of where they come from or their academic pursuits. I have worked alongside many of them and know too many to name, but Nicole Campbell from Western and Alison Flynn from uOttawa need a special shout out! However, like in any system, there are people who come from different paths that may not hold an inclusive view. Some faculty do not care for the "C's get degrees" approach to university studies. Some faculty also don't think students should be working outside of their studies. They should be full-time students. From an equity lens, this is not feasible for many students. They need to work but that doesn't discount their commitment to their studies.

Andrew and I talked frankly that day in the hallway. I did my best to encourage him to persist.

"You, me, or nobody is gonna hit as hard as life. But it ain't about how hard you hit. It's about how hard you can get hit and keep moving forward, how much you can take and keep moving forward."

**SYLVESTER STALLONE
AS ROCKY BALBOA**

"You need to rest, not quit," I said. "Many of us have hit this wall before too. I know what this feels like. I've hit a lot of walls myself. It is when you are getting closer to the finish line, when you are tired, depleted, and the thought of quitting is the only comforting thought you can muster, that you have to find a way to just finish, no matter what. I get it, Andrew, but you need to keep going. You need to regroup, take quitting off the table, and find your way back."

I asked him to reconnect with his "why"—the reason he was there in the first place. He wanted to get the degree so he could be a police officer. I encouraged him to focus hard on that. Andrew listened. And he did end up finishing his degree.

Years later I was happily surprised to hear from Andrew, who was seeking a reference for his police application. He thought I was one of the only people at the university who might remember him. I remembered him, and I was honoured to serve as a reference. Andrew had real skill, follow-through, and discipline. It takes a lot of character to make up your mind, then change it back again. His recruiter and I spent a long time on the phone. I explained how extraordinary it was that Andrew was able to come back from the brink of quitting.

A few months later, I received a lovely note from Andrew when he was hired as a police officer. He achieved his goal. Andrew always seemed able to find his way back.

A few years later, after no contact with Andrew, I received a thank-you card in the mail at the university. Andrew had recently been honoured for his pivotal role in de-escalating a potential high school shooting. Andrew's work saved lives and prevented an unimaginable tragedy. After the award ceremony, Andrew shared that he had been reflecting on how he ended up being a police officer. He recounted a conversation with a high school teacher who told him he would never amount to anything. Reflecting on that teacher who had counted him out apparently brought back our conversation—the opposite message. My heart burst with pride for him.

We reconnected and I learned that, as in most resiliency stories, his life after university was not all smooth sailing. He had setbacks, disappointments, and losses along the way. After he finally became a police officer, he experienced significant challenges from first-hand exposure to trauma, early in his career, after being the first to respond to a youth suicide call. But Andrew was able to come back from that.

What makes Andrew an extraordinary police officer is that he feels. He puts in the time and dedication to acknowledge the shadows and the downs, yet he continues. He came back from a failed police interview, trauma, and many other challenges. And by doing what he does, coming back from adversity, he was where he needed to be to save countless lives that day at the local high school. Oh, and that high school just happened to be the same one where the teacher told him he would never amount to anything. That teacher was still there.

Thankfully for everyone, Andrew did something that that teacher did not believe he could do. He rose to the challenge and succeeded.

"

Your value doesn't decrease
based on someone's inability
to see your worth.

"

CHAPTER 13

WORTH

I N THE INTRODUCTION, I invited you to set your intention for this book. What was it that you were hoping to explore, learn, or discover? Let's take a moment to bring that intention forward again. Was there something in your intention that touched on feelings or emotions? Maybe you wanted to feel something differently or start feeling anything again after a loss. Perhaps you wanted to know more about the origins of these big emotions that seem to hijack your heart and head. Or perhaps you were wondering if other people feel as much as you do, or if other people feel like they are doing resiliency and life wrong. Maybe you just wanted to know a bit more about resiliency in general. Feelings and emotions are usually high on people's list of things they want help understanding and navigating. And there is a connection with how we feel and our sense of worth.

Often when I am working with people, whether it is in large organizations or in one-on-one consulting, I observe patterns or trends that seem to speak more to our shared experience as human beings than the roles or positions we hold. For example, on a phone call this week I was working with a high-level senior executive who routinely makes north of a million dollars a year in salary, and he shared with me that he just does not feel like his work matters. He said that he constantly feels like he is not doing enough. He asked me, "Am I good at my job?" And while talking with a friend over lunch hour, they shared with me that they were feeling stuck in the thinking that their work does not matter. Who actually cares about my children's screen time? they lamented. Does this even matter, Robyne? they asked me pleadingly. Will my parenting be enough? Am I a good enough mom? My after-noon Zoom meeting that day was with a superintendent of a local school district, and they shared that they felt like no one was even going to read their report, anyway, so did their work make a difference? Was it enough to help the students and teachers? Were they the right person for the job? This idea of not being enough comes up time and time again.

In Part II of this book we discussed the external barriers of stress, fear, and stigma and how they relate to resiliency. One additional area that I wanted to explore here for you is the role of our sense of esteem or worth. I see in my work that our sense of esteem and worth impacts how we feel and ulti-mately how we show up in our lives.

I believe there is a relationship between this sense of not doing or being enough in our culture and our capacity for resiliency. We are weary and wobbly from the ever-growing to-do lists compared to the done lists. We are stuck in a pattern of being on auto-pilot for much of our lives, until something goes wrong.

My invitation for you is to take this moment to revisit this idea of being and doing enough and explore the idea of your worth. Is it in the doing, performing, competing, that you feel your worth? Are you trying to earn your sense of worth or your rest? I come upon so many paradoxes in my work. I see people trying to hate themselves healthy. Shame themselves into healing. Self-help themselves into self-esteem. The reality is that we need to stop running ourselves down. We need to stop the constant chasing and start reconnecting with the moment. We need to host a personal mutiny against the whirlpool of thoughts that say we are not doing enough. You are likely doing the best you can with the tools you have. You need to stop the spiral of chasing yourself into value. Otherwise this will deplete you. You will have nothing left in your tank for when life happens. Most people could handle the current adverse event that is happening if they knew their worth and did not drain their emotion reserves needlessly or as frequently.

KNOW YOUR WORTH

One of my friends has known personal loss and tragedy that would bring most people to their knees. He once shared with me there were days when he wished for only garbage and laundry to do. What he meant is that every day when there is something lovely, wonderful, or pleasant—any positive experience, really—his heart breaks because his wife is not here to see it, to share it. And when things are hard, sad, or scary and he desperately needs to be part of a pair, comforted, or held, she is not here either.

So he needs days when nothing extraordinarily good or bad happens, to be able to catch his breath and regain his strength, so when interesting days happen like holidays and important moments, he can push through and be there for his kids. He went on to explain, "That's why I look forward to garbage and laundry days—plain, simple, something I can cope with." My friend learned early on that he needed to have moments that were just okay.

Yet, people constantly try to cheer him up by telling him to find meaning in his losses. When people talk about him, I hear things like, "He is too young to be a widow"; "The children need a mother"; "He will be okay once he finds someone." I believe people share these thinly veiled opinions to alleviate their own discomfort, not his.

What makes my friend's experience with loss so inspiring is that through all of his pain, his sense of worth or worthiness doesn't change. It is steadfast. He knows that life is not punishing him. He knows who he is and what he needs. He operates from a place of constant assurance that he is okay, and it will be okay.

Someone knowing their worth and showing up every day in their life regardless of the hits they take shows the power of our capacity to be resilient and rise.

My friend is not a victim. He is living his life as he sees fit. Tragedy taught him not to listen to all the outside noise. He is unscathed by the people on the sidelines. It is not that he doesn't care about people; he just doesn't care about their opinions of his life. Garbage and laundry days may always serve as his precious sanctuary. I admire him for it.

One of the most challenging things for us to do in life is to know our worth, deep in our bones, and actually believe it. I believe that we knew our worth, or at least did not question it, when we were born. As children we innately know we matter, and we are special. But as we grow, we start to question that core belief: Am I really worthy?

Society has proclaimed that our worth is something that has to be earned, won, or proved. We are supposed to be extraordinary in absolutely every area—in our jobs, our family life, our extracurriculars, and even our personal wellness. This fast-paced rat race of seeking other people's approval is hurting our humanity. It is harder than ever to grasp that deep sense of our worth. Evidence of this is that we can never seem to have enough of what we don't need. Despite all the material things, approvals, and accolades, we feel like something is missing. Because we actually don't need it all, we will never have enough of it, because it is the wrong remedy. The antidote is to reconnect with our self-worth. And to do this, we can start by revisiting the notion of self-esteem. There is a connection between self-esteem and resiliency. We need to believe we deserve to feel well and be okay.

SELF-ESTEEM AS SELF-WORTH

Self-esteem is a billion-dollar industry. Just think of all the things the world is selling you to make you feel better. Society breaks people down through social comparison and then offers the solution. Think of the Axe body products commercials. They portray women as objects, men as gods, and the products as tools to make men irresistible to women. Now, take the Dove line of products. The idea being sold is that women should feel beautiful no matter their size, colour, and shape. The Dove Campaign for Real Beauty wages war against a society that pressures women to look a particular way. Ironically, Dove and Axe are owned by the same parent company, Unilever. Break people and then sell them the remedy. Poor self-esteem is great for capitalism and commercialism. This is why we never feel good enough. Society profits when we hurt, so we keep getting sold more and more things we "need."

To take back our power, we need to revisit how we think of our self-esteem. Gabor Maté's research offers helpful insights into how we can understand this relationship between how we feel and the corporate system.

Maté introduced the idea of contingent self-esteem and genuine self-esteem. Contingent self-esteem relies on circumstances and achievements. He also uses the term "conditional self-worth." The idea is that your sense of worth or self-esteem relies on external forces such as validation or approval so you can feel good about yourself. This is where the majority of people land. Garnering followers, likes, trendy things, big houses, and perfect bodies and families is an attempt to experience the high of contingent self-esteem. The dependence on acceptance and approval from the outside world is why people's sense of worth is so fluctuating, sporadic, and prone to collapse. Maté defines genuine self-esteem or self-worth a consistent, steadfast, and unfluctuating baseline of knowing your worth, which comes from within you rather than from outside. It is always there. Always intact. Maté explains that it is like an oasis within you that provides support and a sense of unconditional self-love, even in difficult times.

To come upon the belief that you are enough as you are, and you can be resilient when called upon, your genuine self-worth must be reclaimed and remembered. Maté refers to this as a return to our inherent wholeness.[1] Another scholar,

Kimberly Miller, sums it up beautifully by explaining that you reclaim your worth when you realize and accept that you are valued and worthy simply by virtue of being you!²

Lesson Learned

On a not particularly exciting June day, I was working in my office at the university when Jaxson's teacher called me. She shared candidly that she was worried because Jaxson was hungry at school. "You need to send him with a proper meal," she said. This phone call felt like I had just got hit in the face with a picnic table. The teacher was kind and considerate, but I felt judged. I couldn't believe I had been so busy with everything else that my little one was hungry at school. My mind raced. Jaxson is our third-born. Of course, he was being neglected. Hunter, the eldest, had gorgeous bento box lunches worthy of social media posts, as did Ava, but not Jaxson. What a quick fall from grace. What kind of mother was I? My mind raced and my emotions plummeted.

I had a few hours left at work, so I put on peaceful music and turned on my diffuser to fill my office with scents of lavender, lemongrass, and rainwater. Nothing changed. I started rubbing the essential oils all over my hands, neck, and temples. Nothing happened. I came quickly to my first realization. Essential oils just make your problems smell better. My office was radiating Zen, but on the inside, I was spiralling.

Opposite-action time! When you are spiralling and feeling awful, immediately take opposite action—in other words, do the opposite of what you are feeling. I was feeling helpless and guilty, so my opposite actions were to make a plan and make amends ASAP. My new plan: Drive home, beat the school bus, surprise Jaxson coming home from school, declare my love for him as a third-born and promise to make him his favourite dinner and lunches for a month, apologize to him for not having a baby book of him, offer him the USB memory stick that has most of his baby pictures, and remind him that he is not here as "spare parts" for his brother or sister if they ever have a medical emergency.

Yes, that is what he needs to hear, I thought to myself. Well, that is exactly what I did. I unleashed my opposite-action plan on an innocent Jaxson, just coming home from school. Yeah, he didn't see that coming! It started with "Surprise, mama's home early!" and ended with "You are not 'spare parts' for a medical emergency!" Just as I'd planned.

Thankfully Jaxson is an easygoing, fun-loving joy of a child, who despite his great surprise looked deep into my eyes, tilted his head, and kindly asked, "Are you okay? What is all this about?" Ava seemed unfazed, wondered out loud if I had just listened to a new book or podcast, and proceeded to get ready for gymnastics. Jaxson, on the other hand, really wanted to know if I was okay. I shared with him that his teacher had told me he was hungry at school. Jaxson said that that morning he had been in a rush, so he took only a bunch of the little muffins I had made yesterday for his lunch and snacks. "Mama, the other kids really loved your muffins, so I shared them. That's why I was hungry today. It is not a big deal."

I suddenly went from feeling like a horrible, no-good, rotten mama to an excited mother bursting with joy at the news. "You mean the other kids liked my muffins?" I shrieked. I instantly felt overwhelmed with pride and a deep sense accomplishment. *Yes!* I thought to myself. *The other kids loved my muffins! Win for me!* Then I paused. *Good grief! Hold the phone here, Robyne,* I thought to myself. *I just went 180 degrees emotionally in under ten seconds flat. Not okay . . .*

When your thoughts, emotions, and behaviour are bouncing around like a pinball, pause. Take a deep breath and ask yourself, "What story am I telling myself right now?" The story I had been telling myself all afternoon, since the teacher had called, was that I was a neglectful, busy professional mother who was dropping the ball all the time. I was not doing life well enough. I was letting down my kids. I could not manage my career and a family. I was a joke.

But as soon as I heard that the other kids liked my muffins (contingent self-esteem boosting), I felt elated. The world somehow validated me through other kids liking my muffins! Note to self: My self-worth ought not to be determined by other children liking my muffins! Thankfully, the trust in Jaxson's eyes when he asked me if I was truly okay showed he knows his mama's worth is not connected to bento box lunches.

When we focus on the outside world and depend on it for our sense of worth, our inside world is chaotic. It is hard to keep up. It feels so inauthentic. Our self-esteem always feels fleeting and temporary. Our self-worth depends on how well the world thinks we are doing—and the world's judgement is not kind. So, to keep mindfulness and reclaiming your self-worth practical and sustainable, be sure to check in often about the stories you are telling yourself. If you come upon the realization that the stories are not kind, here is a small exercise you can try to rewrite those stories.

1   **Identify the false belief by name.** Shine a light on it. Name it. Maybe you notice that you say to yourself that you do not deserve this positive outcome or to be happy: the false belief there is "I am not worthy." Or perhaps you tell yourself that you are not enough: the false belief is "I don't belong." Another example could be, "I am too emotional or crazy": the false belief is "I am defective."

2 **Dissolving and redefining.** This is when you take on the role as an observer by being a detective. Where is the evidence for this false belief? Where did it come from? The goal is to identity the origins, if you can, demystify the feeling, and try to move to facts. For example, "I am not athletic": okay, so you do not see yourself as an athlete, but where is the judgement coming from? Can you pull apart the feeling from the fact? Are athletes in your definition only one body type? Can you broaden your definitions? Start looking for evidence of what an athlete is in a more holistic manner. Another example is "I am ashamed of my mistakes," which has the undertone of the false belief that you are your mistakes or are permanently fractured. Okay, so you *made* a mistake—you are not the mistake. As I shared before, mistakes are events, not characteristics. The idea is to dissolve the belief from the feeling through fact-finding. And if the fact does lead to the conclusion that the belief is not false, then you have a choice. Are you going to stay stuck there or are you going to do something about it? As Hunter likes to remind me, "If you are not willing to work for it, don't complain about not having it." Oh, the wisdom of teenagers!

3 **Create the new experiences or evidence.** The idea is that if you do not have facts that help dissolve the false belief, then create them. Forge new experiences and evidence to support more helpful beliefs about yourself. Sticking with the example "I am not an athlete," the goal is to create a broader definition of "athlete" or to find ways of expressing a positive belief, such as "I am someone who enjoys movement" or "I am someone who appreciates being strong and flexible." To strengthen the belief, be sure to

say it out loud. It is helpful to have our minds and ears hear more supportive messaging.

Aspire for those stories to come from within, not from society. At the beginning of this book, I shared with you the parts of my story that contributed to my broken sense of self. Ultimately, we must feel and know we deserve to be well. We must pay attention to our stories because their tone is connected to our self-worth. Let the stories reaffirm and honour your genuine self-esteem. We can be appreciably kinder to ourselves if we tell our own stories. Spend time reconnecting to the self-worth originating from your own heart. This quote helps keep this idea front of mind: "I know what I bring to the table, so trust me when I say, I'm not afraid to eat alone" (author unknown).

Remember, by virtue of you being here, your worth is already perfectly intact. Visit that oasis inside your soul that already knows this is the truth. You deserve to live within the truth of knowing your worth. Resiliency flourishes when we know we are worthy of being well and deserve to rise again.

THE BIG IDEAS OF PART IV

In Part IV, I introduced the four paths in the form of my Resiliency Trajectory Model. Starting with a baseline of resiliency made up of the five pillars, a person then faces an adverse event. It can be a sudden wallop or a gradual erosion. The key here is that you take that hit. The event or experience requires an action on your part to get back to being okay. You need to rally from this. The word "resiliency" comes from the Latin *resiliens*—"to rebound or recoil." The event must have enough impact to knock you down; then, it is up to you to get back up. Another way of looking at it is through the analogy of a bow and arrow. An arrow can be shot only by first pulling it backward. That is how it gains momentum. We first go back, then move forward, stronger.

The first path is the decline phase. You take the hit. It hurts. Perhaps you are feeling a little shell-shocked or numb. Maybe you are in disbelief that this is happening. Next, you shift into the adapt phase. Life will go on. It is unfair and cruel that the world does not even stop for a moment to let you catch your breath, but the adapt phase is when you learn new ways of being. The pain coexists while we grow. Next comes the reclaim phase, when you start to take on that new learning or new way of being as part of your reality. You may not like it, but it is here, and you persist. The last path is the rise phase. You are far enough on the other side of the adverse event that you can see you are going to be okay. You have navigated another life event.

This reminds me of an old saying that goes something like this: ships don't sink because of the water around them; they sink because of the water that gets in them. While the meaning of this saying is a reminder to not let what is happening around you get inside you and weigh you down, I think it can also reference the rise phase after an adverse event. When we make it this far, we see that the water is not coming into our boat. We are not going to sink: we are going to make it after all. We are going to be okay.

In chapter 1, I came out the gates quickly with my own story of resiliency. I shared with you my fear that I may not have been worthy of my rescue. Back then, I struggled with my feelings of not deserving my miracle. And now I have the good fortune to work with so many people who have experienced both the worst and the best of life. Some of these people share with me that they too questioned their bounce-back. They too were left wondering why they had survived. The only antidote to this type of question, in my opinion, is to accept that our worth is not determined by our morality. We need to change the subtle script that tells us if we are good, we deserve this positive outcome, and if we are a bad person, we deserve this negative outcome. We need to accept that life happens, and it is not for us to understand all the moving parts. If we are here, we still have work to do. Our worth is intact as it is. We all hold worth in equal part as global citizens on this third rock from the sun.

LIGHTHOUSES

LIGHTHOUSES ARE MY favourite type of structure in the world. I am spellbound by their grandeur, beauty, strength, and purpose. Lighthouses have the most hopeful and spectacular vistas on earth, complete openness and vastness of the waters outstretched at their feet. Wherever I travel in the world, I always try to find the lighthouses. Jeff can attest to the lengths I will go!

Case in point: One June, we trekked down to Prince Edward Island (PEI) a few days before my conference started at the University of PEI. With such endearing enthusiasm, my husband joined me as we spent two full days driving around the island in search of the sixty-three lighthouses! We found nearly every one. I suspect that the car rental people were shocked by how many kilometers we put on that car without ever leaving the island, given that PEI is only 225 kilometres long and 65 kilometres wide at its largest points! We travelled almost every inch of that island—through little muddy cow paths to the farthest northern tip to the most southern point, to the most eastern lighthouses and back to West Point, we took in every lighthouse we could find, big and small. Point Prim, Howards Cove, Panmure Island, Souris, East Point, West Point, and the North Cape. My heart was completely enraptured by the history and the stories I imagined those lighthouses held within their towers.

Lighthouses bring me an inexplicable sense of comfort and safety, and the deepest sense of connection I have to my ancestors. My ancestors left Scotland aboard the SS *Rambler*, which landed on June 20, 1806, in PEI, as a result of the Highland Clearances. My other ancestors survived the brutal Clearances by moving to Glasgow for a time, but they eventually fled to Canada in 1926 aboard the SS *Montnairn*, which landed in Montreal on October 15. My grandfather was a child when he and his brave young parents and small siblings left Port Glasgow. While standing on the deck, his father, James Joseph, encouraged him to take "a long and strong look," as this would be the last time he would ever see his grandparents or homeland again. Upon arriving at the Old Port of Montreal, he would have seen the newly built Sailor's Memorial Clock, which also served as the lighthouse guiding him to his new home. My paternal relatives made their way to Galt, Ontario, while my maternal relatives, descendants from the Stewarts and the Campbells of Murray Harbour, PEI, stayed for generations. Although they were farmers, their lives intertwined with the sea and the lighthouses. My grandfather worked aboard the ferry, shuttling people from PEI to Nova Scotia. He shared with me that children on the Island didn't count sheep when they were trying to fall asleep, they could count the light beams from the Murray Harbour Range lighthouse. My mother would spend summers in PEI after her family moved to Ontario. My parents eventually found their way back to life on the water, and my dad promptly built a small replica lighthouse, which proudly sits at the end of their dock. Lighthouses are how we find our way home.

YOUR LIGHTHOUSES

Over the course of this book, I have aspired to share with you my ideas about resiliency and how we can navigate the ever-changing landscape of our lives. Now I will help you find your lighthouses. The lighthouse analogy can serve as a cue to think about what we look out for and pay attention to. From what do you draw direction, connection, strength, and focus in your life?

I like to think that we all could benefit if we carried lighthouses in our hearts.

My grandfather used to say that the storms disappear once you see the lighthouse. Our lives will inevitably be filled with storms, setbacks, and challenges. If your life is hard, it is not because you are doing it wrong or there is something wrong with you. Life is just hard. There is absolutely no easy way out. We are all descendants of tribes of people who long ago knew this truth. We are all indigenous to somewhere. And in that somewhere, life was hard too, probably even more so, and they persisted. It is helpful to pause and truly explore your family's story. You are part of a long line of people who have walked the earth. It is when we reconnect with our own origin stories that we can see our deepest belonging. Knowing your story is extremely powerful. Your people made it. They rallied. They persisted. They survived and you are here as living proof.

"Once the lighthouse is seen, the rest of the sea is ignored."

TERRI GUILLEMETS

Remember, it is only recently, as we have become more settled and comfortable, that as a society we do not like hard. We are told that we should not ever be in discomfort. This is simply not true or possible. This idea that we should avoid hard things or challenges is robbing us of our potential and hurting our sense of worth. Each one of us has the capacity within our life today to reclaim our personal sense of being enough. We will survive challenges just as our ancestors did. We are brave and courageous in the face of uncertainty and change. We will continue to thrive, grow, fail, learn, try again, fall, hurt, rally, reclaim, and rise. We are enough. We have always been enough just by virtue of our existence.

My invitation is for you to map out your lighthouses. This will create a clear vision of where you want to go and sharpen your focus. Where you put your focus, your energy will follow. What guiding messages do you want to establish that will be your focus points as you navigate your world? Through the storms, we can choose where we look and what we cling to for guidance and safety. You are welcome to borrow some of my focus points, which I have included below to get you started, but I do encourage you to discover what speaks to you personally.

My Lighthouses

The italicized phrase serves as my lighthouse, my reminder when life gets difficult.

When life is hard: *I can do hard things.*

When I am scared to change: *A boat is safe in the harbour, but that is not the purpose of a boat.*

When I don't feel like it: *Goals don't work if you do them only on days when you feel like it.*

When I am overwhelmed: *All will be well.*

When I am tired: *Rest, don't quit.*

When I am afraid: *Feel the fear and do it anyway.*

When I am ashamed and embarrassed: *"I loved you at your darkest."* (Romans 5:8)

When the storms of life are scary and unpredictable: *The sun is shining above the clouds.* Tomorrow will be here before I know it. Trust.

When I feel like I'm failing as a mom: *I am the only mother they have.* It's not about how much I do; it's about how much I love.

When I need to be brave: *"God is within her; she will not fail."* (Psalms 46:5)

When I want to stop running: *Embrace the suck.* I run to celebrate movement, not as self-punishment.

When I am being hard on myself: *You cannot hate yourself healthy.*

When I miss my mom: Mizpah *(Hebrew word for connection, the emotional bond between two people apart).* I will see her again.

When life is so good it hurts: *Thank you.* Thank you. Thank you. (Good things come in threes!)

Now, take a moment to explore what speaks to you. When feelings and events present themselves as you embark on each new day, what will you focus on? What will guide you?

What will become your lighthouse? I have done this practice for so long, and my brain is so conditioned to this line of thinking, that it almost feels automatic. In neuropsychology we talk about how repetitive thoughts create grooves in our brains. Every thought you have is a chemical reaction that travels through a channel made up of receptors and connectors. As the reaction travels along this route, we experience awareness. Research has demonstrated that when a particular thought is repeated frequently, the pathway forms a groove. What is so amazing about this grooving is that future thoughts automatically will return to the familiar grooves. This is why patterned thinking feels so engrained. It literally is carving out grooves in our brain matter. But thankfully, with intention and repetition we can create new grooves, and as those new grooves get used more, the old grooves fade.

My hope for you is that eventually your lighthouses become natural, like a reflex. When life happens, your mind will recall your new way of seeing the world so quickly that your lighthouses will feel like an old friend, or a special ancestor, giving you strong and tender comforting words that let you know you can keep going: *All will be well. We've got you. You do not walk alone.*

FIND YOUR "WHY" AND YOU WILL FIND YOUR WAY

Earlier in the book, I shared the profound wisdom of Viktor Frankl, the psychiatrist who survived the Holocaust and introduced his theory of logotherapy to the world. Frankl explained that we cannot avoid suffering but we can choose how to find meaning, how to cope, and how to push forward. It is important to note that finding meaning is not the same thing as finding a silver lining in every suffering. Sometimes, there is no silver lining. The heart of logotherapy is the belief that we need to find meaning that speaks to us personally—what is meaningful depends on us. The aim here is not to find meaning by asking "why" questions; rather, finding your "why" means finding your purpose, being mindful of what something means to you and how you will act accordingly. Frankl wrote, "Life is never made unbearable by circumstances, but only by lack of meaning and purpose." He encourages us to keep an open heart in the face of challenges and suffering: "In some ways suffering ceases to be suffering at the moment it finds a meaning, such as the meaning of a sacrifice."[1]

While I was hospitalized for a brief time as a teenager, I was convinced that my problems, or, more appropriately, my lack of problems, in comparison to others, seemed pathetic. Who was I to feel so much darkness when I had so much support and love? I remember reading this Frankl passage:

> To draw an analogy: a man's suffering is similar to the behavior of a gas. If a certain quantity of gas is pumped into an empty chamber, it will fill the chamber completely and evenly, no matter how big the chamber. Thus, suffering completely fills the human soul and conscious mind, no matter whether the suffering is great or little. Therefore the "size" of human suffering is absolutely relative.[2]

My pain filled my entire world and coming upon this realization helped me accept that my pain was real enough to hurt as bad as it did. Whatever hurts you, hurts you; whatever troubles you, troubles you. It is all real. Judging it or questioning it will not serve you.

I recently worked with a group of emergency room physicians in Nova Scotia. There had been a murderous rampage across the province. Several local communities were impacted and there was a significant loss of life. One of the doctors shared with me that she felt bad for feeling so distraught, because some of her colleagues were impacted more than she had been. This was other people's grief, she felt. What right did she have to feel so sad?

Again, if we look at Frankl's analogy, we understand that whether something terrible directly impacts us or we are proxy to it, our suffering is real. The wise approach is to carry it and then choose how we will use it in a meaningful way. This is up to you! You get to set the course of what you want to live for. You get to decide what matters most.

I remain awe-inspired that the same man who endured suffering beyond human comprehension in the concentration camps also wrote about the importance of forgiveness and love: "I do not forget any good deed done to me, and I do not carry a grudge for a bad one."[3] This is the ultimate in resiliency. Frankl beautifully concluded his work about human suffering by writing about the importance of love.

As you know, I believe in the human capacity to be resilient. I believe each one of us can draw upon internal wisdom to overcome any circumstance. Frankl is a perfect example of this. His work and writing planted the seed of resiliency in my heart when I thought all hope was gone. His legacy for me is how I see the world with lighthouses. And for that, I want to share his work as broadly as I can. His book *Man's Search for Meaning* will always be my favourite on the topic of resiliency.

YOUR NEXT ADVENTURE

My last intention is to set you upon your next adventure. To do so, I will leave you with my favourite question, asked by Mr. Buckminster Fuller in 1983. Fuller was a revolutionary. He was a brilliant scientist, artist, visionary, and inventor. He asked the world tough questions, kindly, in the hope of making the world better. This was the question that I heard as a battle cry for sharing everyday resiliency practices with you, the catalyst to writing this very book. But it serves as an open call to action for all of us:

"What is my job on the planet? What is it that needs doing that I know something about, that probably won't happen unless I take responsibility for it?"[4]

When you find your answer, you will also find your next adventure. Go bravely and trust that you are well equipped. Reconnect to your roots to find where you truly belong. Be flexible and nimble as the road changes to meet you. Accept what is and know that what happens next is always up to you. Embrace and nurture a hopeful heart in all that you do. And be mindful of the wonder and pockets of joy tucked away in life's moments that are waiting for you to discover them.

And know that in your bones, you are already enough. Let this message create an emotional echo in your being that never ends. You can do hard things. See every part of your life through this lens: *I can do hard things.* Awaken this truth. Hold it close.

You are worthy of all your bounce-backs.

You can reset, restart, and recalibrate as many times as you need to.

You are well equipped in this very moment.

You can trust in yourself that you will be okay tomorrow.

My hope for you is that you can let go of what no longer serves you.

That you can coexist with the parts you are not yet ready to let go of.

That you pick your battles based on what is worth fighting for.

And that you find your calm within any storm.

ACKNOWLEDGEMENTS

A BOOK ADVENTURE IS only possible because of the people who surround us and support us: our families, teachers, colleagues, guides, friends, and clearly our pets. So, with a grateful heart, I express my deep gratitude with these acknowledgements. And if you happen to listen to the *Gladiator* movie soundtrack as you read these words, you might just shed a tear. I did. I cried the whole time writing this!

Thank you to my brilliant team at Page Two. It was such an honour being guided by such strong and talented women. Kindness and confidence are their superpowers. Thank you to my Page Two mastermind, Trena White. You shared your world and your team with me so generously. Thank you, Amanda Lewis, for being my editorial compass. I spent many hours behind my computer screen in full conversation with your "AL comments and suggestions"! I love that I could make you laugh, and you told me exactly where you laughed. You have changed my relationship with Track Changes for the better. Thank you, Janet, Taysia, and Caela for your work too. I am clearly the rookie on this team, but I have grown because of these thoughtful and skilled people. I can confidently say I am now an emerging writer. (Side note: if you ever have a wild dream, tell someone. I did just that. Just casually, in passing, I mentioned to my friend Martin that I was entertaining this wild and scary idea of writing a non-academic book. Well, thanks to Martin, here I am writing my book under Page Two!)

My deepest gratitude to you, Farah and Martin Perelmuter, for introducing me to your big, bright, and exciting world of Speakers' Spotlight. I am the rookie in this domain as well. Thank you for your support, guidance, and insight. Because of you two, I am working with people and companies I ever only hoped to share my work with. Thank you for keeping a watchful eye on me and helping me learn the ropes. I feel supported and valued. Thank you for believing in my work. And thank you to everyone at Speakers, past and present, for giving me a chance! I also express my heartfelt thanks to the thousands of people I have met through my work with Speakers who boldly shared their stories with me. Thank you to the strangers who told me they know my mom is proud of me. Your words are healing my tender heart.

I have met and worked with so many people in my travels who have made such an impact on my work and my understanding of resiliency. I wish I could hold space for all of you here and thank you publicly. I think because I take off my armour when I present my work on resiliency, others return the favour. Thank you to everyone for the candid conversations and trusting me with parts of your stories at the front of stages, in airports, in classrooms, at conferences, in Zoom chats, in hallways, in follow-up emails, or as we walked to the parking lot. I hold them close. A special thank-you to Cavell Johnson, Clint and Joan Malarchuk, and Tonia Jahshan, who shared their journeys so boldly and helped me find my confidence to just be me on those stages. Thank you also to the brilliant speakers, like Ron Tite, Dr. Greg Wells, and Melissa Leong, who generously share lessons from the trenches backstage with this rookie. And thank you to gifted singer-songwriter Peter Katz. Part IV of this book was written to his albums on repeat. Peter also happened to give our daughter, Ava, a virtual personalized grade eight graduation concert when COVID-19 had her graduating in our living room over Zoom. Bravo to you all and thank you.

I also want to thank the wonderful world of educators. Educators are like my super-cozy hoodie. No matter what, the fit is just right. Despite me being an elementary school teacher for a fraction of a second, I do view my fellow educators as my people. I have met enough teachers, like Laura Cipolla, Mark Astrom, Claire Mooney, Janet Muir, Dana Stanlick, and Jenny Chen, to patch over the hurts of past teachers. I believe in teachers again because of the remarkable people I see in classrooms all around Canada. I have a special place in my heart for Bluewater District School Board and Sheryl Elliott, and the BC district school boards. Thank you for the work you do. I would also like to express my appreciation of and gratitude for the academic institutions that opened their doors to me. Thank you, Trent, Queen's, and Western universities for the post-secondary learning adventures. And the biggest academic thank-you needs to go to St. Lawrence College in Kingston, Ontario. That college gave me a chance even with messy and cobbled-together high school transcripts. I found my academic voice and footing at SLC, and that empowered me to go check out a few other schools after my time in Kingston!

I would also like to acknowledge the hundreds of students I have had the honour of learning alongside. To my students who challenge, inspire, and welcome me into the classroom, thank you. And to my colleagues who became friends: Rich, Stephanie, Lily, Michael J., Fergal, and Aleyah. Thank you also to my students-turned-police-officers, Andrew and Mackenzie. A special acknowledgement to the strongest and bravest student I ever had the privilege of teaching, Alissa: you inspire me. You are our chosen family now, Alissa. We love you dearly.

Thank you to our friends who have supported all of us while also sharing coffee, tears, laughter, carpools, and sports stories. A special thank-you to the DiBellas and the Keast family. I count you all as blessings.

A special shout-out goes to the creators and authors who have shared their ideas and gifts with the world. To the imagined-into-life heroes like Rocky, Uhtred, Anne Shirley, and Jane Eyre, and to the real-life heroes like Elizabeth Manley, Arlene Dickinson, Jann Arden, Rudy Ruettiger, Vince Papale, Hans Zimmer, and Alanis Morissette: thank you for lending me courage.

Thanks go to the little but mighty Hanley and Stewart clans. I recognize the strong women and men of my family who braved challenges and faced adversity while raising families. I am grateful for the privilege that I am afforded because of their sacrifices in coming to Canada. As with all clans, we are made up of a larger group that are composed of so many people who are very dear to me. I want to thank all the Pollacks, Grattons, Stewarts, and the Bistritans, Burnetts, Youngs, Klassens, Woodys, Epps, Hanleys, and the next generations. Although we may be many miles apart, I hold you close in my heart. I am also deeply indebted to my aunts who rallied around me when I lost my mom. Thank you for helping me remember how she lived and how she loved me.

And of course, I want to thank my home team: my parents, Michael and Lesley. I am deeply proud to be their daughter. Thank you, Dad, for being my constant. You are my witness to my whole life so far. You walked with me in the valleys and along mountaintops. I have shared some the world's most stunning vistas with you and because of you. Dad, you are brave, humble, wise, thoughtful, and loyal. Thank you for the lessons, the chats, the boat rides, and for sharing your gift of storytelling with me. Thank you for carrying me during the times when I was weak and for always giving me second chances. I hope I can make you as proud of me as I am of you. Mom: when we see each other again, over a cup of tea, I have a lifetime of stories to share with you. Please know I have carried you with me in every moment.

To my husband, Jeff: you were heaven-sent. No doubt about that. We found one another when I needed you most and you have never left my side. Your integrity and your commitment to this family is to be lauded. I love that we are in this circus together, and that you assure me every day by your words and actions you would run away with me again, given the chance! I pick you every time. Thank you for being my husband. "If my last words are not 'I love you,' ye'll ken it was because I didna have time."

And lastly, to my mighty three—my personal March Madness —Hunter, Ava Lesley, and Jaxson: being a mom to you three is the biggest and brightest blessing in my life. You are my true joy. Seeing the world from your perspective gives me hope for the future. Each one of your futures is bright in its own unique way. Hunter: you are in a league of your own. I know what we have is something special. You are the real deal. Believe the hype. You are going places, my boy. Ava Lesley: I am so glad that I have one daughter and it is you! I am so proud of the person you are and the strength you carry. You are a big deal in our family. You are our one and only Ava! And to Jax-i-boy: your smile is my kryptonite. You are such an interesting and fun person. You carved out that last chamber in my heart and completed our family. So, you three, keep your siblinghood close and protect it. It is the longest season of your lives. You three can weather any storm. (PS: Hunter: 44, Ava: 50, and Jaxson: 54—that is how many times I mentioned your names in this book . . . you don't have to count! I love you all completely and uniquely.)

And to you, dear reader, as I shared earlier in this book, our paths have now crossed. I am glad you are here. Thank you for sharing your time with my book. I cannot wait for our paths to cross again. Until next time. Take good care and be well.

Sláinte!

NOTES

Introduction: Truly Okay

1   Betsy Kaplan, "Ram Dass: We're All Just Walking Each Other Home," Connecticut Public Radio, January 9, 2020, wnpr.org/post/ram-dass-were-all-just-walking-each-other-home.

Chapter 1: The Sentence

1   World Health Organization, "Social Determinants of Health," WHO, who.int/social_determinants/en/.

2   Goodreads, s.v. "Maya Angelou Quotes," goodreads.com/quotes/7273813-do-the-best-you-can-until-you-know-better-then.

Chapter 2: Resiliency Redefined

1   Elizabeth Azide, "The Philosophy of Resilience," *The Philosophy of Everything* (blog), September 25, 2017, thephilosophyofeverything.com/blog/2017/9/25/the-philosophy-of-resilience.

2   Quotefancy, s.v. "Seneca Quotes," quotefancy.com/seneca-quotes.

3   Christopher Munsey, "The Veterans Who Transformed Psychology," *American Psychological Association* 41, no. 10 (November 2010): apa.org/monitor/2010/11/veterans.

4   P. Alex Linley, Stephen Joseph, Susan Harrington, and Alex Wood, "Positive Psychology: Past, Present, and (Possible) Future," *Journal of Positive Psychology* 1, no. 1 (2006): doi.org/10.1080/17439760500372796.

5   Lolly Bowean, "Obama Hopes His Presidential Center Will Transform Chicago's South Side," *Chicago Tribune*, October 29, 2019, chicagotribune. com/politics/ct-barack-obama-speaks-summit-20191030-j2bgwsddvfh 3hewkiozb5cjf3y-story.html.

6   Erin Vogel, Jason Rose, Lindsay Roberts, and Katheryn Eckles, "Social Comparison, Social Media, and Self-Esteem," *Psychology of Popular Media Culture* 3, no. 4 (2014): doi.org/10.1037/ppm0000047.

7   Goodreads, s.v. "Viktor Frankl Quotes," goodreads.com/quotes/909416-ever-more-people-today-have-the-means-to-live-but.

8   JmStorm (@storm_jon), Twitter, January 12, 2019, 5:48 p.m., twitter.com/storm_jon/status/1084220647960690690.

9   Goodreads, s.v. "Seneca Quotes," goodreads.com/quotes/7441529-there-are-more-things-likely-to-frighten-us-than-there.

Chapter 3: Stress

1   Susan Crompton, "What's Stressing the Stressed? Main Sources of Stress among Workers," Statistics Canada, October 13, 2011, www150.statcan. gc.ca/n1/pub/11-008-x/2011002/article/11562-eng.htm.

2   Canadian Mental Health Association, "The Relationship between Mental Health, Mental Illness and Chronic Physical Conditions," CMHA, ontario. cmha.ca/documents/the-relationship-between-mental-health-mental-illness-and-chronic-physical-conditions/.

3   Glennon Doyle, *Untamed* (New York: Dial, 2020).

4   In Carl Halvor Teigen, "Yerkes-Dodson: A Law for All Seasons," *Theory and Psychology* 4, no. 4 (1994): doi.org/10.1177/0959354394044004.

5   Kelly McGonigal, *The Upside of Stress: Why Stress Is Good for You and How to Get Good at It* (New York: Avery, 2015).

6   Alia Crum, Peter Salovey, and Shawn Achor, "Rethinking Stress: The Role of Mindsets in Determining the Stress Response," *Journal of Personality and Social Psychology* 104, no. 4 (2013): doi.org/10.1037/a0031201.

7   Michael J. Poulin, Stephanie L. Brown, Amanda J. Dillard, and Dylan M. Smith, "Giving to Others and the Association between Stress and Mortality," *American Journal of Public Health* 103, no. 9 (September 2013): doi. org/10.2105/AJPH.2012.300876.

Chapter 4: Fear

1   P. Watson, "What People Usually Fear," *Sunday Times* [London], October 7, 1973. The study cited was R. H. Bruskin Associates, "What Are Americans Afraid Of?" *The Bruskin Report* 53, July 1973.

2   Karen Kangas Dwyer and Marlina M. Davidson, "Is Public Speaking Really Feared More Than Death?" *Communication Research Reports* 29, no. 2 (April 2012): doi.org/10.1080/08824096.2012.667772.

3   Sylco Hoppenbrouwers, Eric Bulten, and Inti Brazil, "Parsing Fear: A Reassessment of the Evidence for Fear Deficits in Psychopathy," *Psychological Bulletin* 142, no. 6 (2016): doi.org/10.1037/bul0000040.

4   Julio Agustin with Kathleen Potts, *The Professional Actor's Handbook: From Casting Call to Curtain Call* (Lanham, MD: Rowman & Littlefield, 2017).

5   Karl Albrecht, "The (Only) 5 Fears We All Share," *BrainSnacks* (newsletter), *Psychology Today*, March 22, 2012, psychologytoday.com/ca/blog/brainsnacks/201203/the-only-5-fears-we-all-share.

6   Cheryl Strayed, *Wild: From Lost to Found on the Pacific Crest Trail* (New York: Knopf, 2012).

7   BrainyQuote, s.v. "Nido Qubein Quotes," brainyquote.com/quotes/nido_qubein_178331.

8   George R. R. Martin, *A Game of Thrones* (New York: Bantam, 1996).

9   Benjamin Mee, *We Bought a Zoo: The Amazing True Story of a Young Family, a Broken-Down Zoo, and the 200 Wild Animals That Changed Their Lives Forever* (New York: Weinstein, 2008).

10 Tim Ferriss, "Fear-Setting: The Most Valuable Exercise I Do Every Month," *Tim Ferriss* (blog), May 15, 2017, tim.blog/2017/05/15/fear-setting/.

11 "Business Advice Quotes by Dale Carnegie," Dale Carnegie: How to Win Friends and Influence People, Strategies for Influence, strategiesforinfluence.com/dale-carnegie-how-to-win-friends-and-influence-people/.

12 Goodreads, s.v. "Anaïs Nin Quotes," goodreads.com/quotes/2061-life-shrinks-or-expands-in-proportion-to-one-s-courage.

Chapter 5: Stigma

1   Steven Neuberg, Dylan M. Smith, and Terrilee Asher, "Why People Stigmatize: Toward a Biocultural Framework," in *The Social Psychology of Stigma*, ed. T. F. Heatherton et al. (New York: Guilford Press, 2000).

2   Patrick W. Corrigan and John R. O'Shaughnessy, "Changing Mental Illness Stigma as It Exists in the Real World," *Australian Psychologist* 42, no. 2 (2007): doi.org/10.1080/00050060701280573.

3   Patrick W. Corrigan and Deepa Rao, "On the Self-Stigma of Mental Illness: Stages, Disclosure, and Strategies for Change," *Canadian Journal of Psychiatry* 57, no. 8 (2012): doi.org/10.1177/070674371205700804.

4   Brené Brown, *The Gifts of Imperfection: Let Go of Who You Think You're Supposed to Be and Embrace Who You Are* (City Center, MN: Hazelden, 2012).

5   Ibid.

Chapter 6: Belonging

1   Goodreads, s.v. "Brené Brown Quotes," goodreads.com/quotes/887653 -those-who-have-a-strong-sense-of-love-and-belonging.

2   Dan Buettner, "The Secrets of Long Life," *National Geographic*, November 2005; scanned magazine pages available at bluezones.com/wp-content/ uploads/2015/01/Nat_Geo_LongevityF.pdf.

3   A thorough examination of attachment theory can be found in Mary D. Salter Ainsworth, Mary C. Blehar, Everett Waters, and Sally N. Wall, *Patterns of Attachment: A Psychological Study of the Strange Situation*, classic ed. (New York: Psychology Press, 2015).

4   An excellent read on this topic is Sue Gerhardt's *Why Love Matters: How Affection Shapes a Baby's Brain* (New York: Routledge, 2014).

5   Michael Carlie, *Into the Abyss: A Personal Journey into the World of Street Gangs*, originally self-published in 2002. The book is now available online here: people.missouristate.edu/MichaelCarlie/site_map.htm.

6   Naomi Eisenberger and Matthew Lieberman, "Why It Hurts to Be Left Out: The Neurocognitive Overlap between Physical and Social Pain," in *The Social Outcast*, ed. Kipling D. Williams et al. (New York: Psychology Press, 2005). PDF available here: researchgate.net/publi cation/237332217_Why_It_Hurts_to_Be_Left_Out_The_Neurocognitive_ Overlap_Between_Physical_and_Social_Pain.

7   Samuel Taylor Coleridge, *The Rime of the Ancient Mariner*, originally published in 1798. Full text of 1834 edition available on Poetry Foundation, poetryfoundation.org/poems/43997/the-rime-of-the-ancient-mariner-text-of-1834.

8   Matthew Lieberman and Naomi Eisenberger, "The Pains and Pleasures of Social Life: A Social Cognitive Neuroscience Approach," *NeuroLeadership Journal*, 2008, www.scn.ucla.edu/pdf/Pains&Pleasures(2008).pdf.

9   Maarten van Doorn, "You Are the Average of the Five People You Spend the Most Time With," Medium, June 20, 2018, medium.com/the-polymath-project/you-are-the-average-of-the-five-people-you-spend-the-most-time-with-a2ea32d08c72.

Chapter 7: Perspective

1   Barbara Coloroso, *Kids Are Worth It! Raising Resilient, Responsible, Compassionate Kids*, revised ed. (Toronto: Penguin Canada, 2010).

2   Marc Jambon, Sheri Madigan, André Plamondon, Ella Daniel, and Jennifer Jenkins, "The Development of Empathic Concern in Siblings: A Reciprocal Influence Model," *Child Development* 90, no. 5 (October 2019): doi.org/10.1111/cdev.13015.

Chapter 8: Acceptance

1   Michael J. Fox, *Always Looking Up: The Adventures of an Incurable Optimist* (New York: Hyperion, 2009).

2   Hayley Phelan, "What's All This about Journaling?" *New York Times*, October 25, 2018, nytimes.com/2018/10/25/style/journaling-benefits.html.

3   Julia Cameron, "Morning Pages," The Artist's Way (website), juliacameronlive.com/basic-tools/morning-pages/.

4   Centre for Addiction and Mental Health, "Dialectical Behavior Therapy," CAMH, camh.ca/en/health-info/mental-illness-and-addiction-index/dialectical-behaviour-therapy.

5   Wendy De Rosa, "21 Powerful Quotes You Need to Hear about Healing, Growing and Living Intuitively," Wendy De Rosa School of Intuitive Studies, schoolofintuitivestudies.com/21-powerful-quotes-you-need-to-hear-about-healing-growing-and-living-intuitively/.

Chapter 9: Hope

1 L. S. Vygotsky, *The Collected Works of L. S. Vygotsky*, ed. Robert Rieber and Aaron Carton, vol. 1: *Problems of General Psychology: Including the Volume Thinking and Speech* (New York: Plenum, 1987).

2 Adam W. Hanley, Alia R. Warner, Vincent M. Dehili, Angela I. Canto, and Eric L. Garland, "Washing the Dishes to Wash the Dishes: Brief Instruction in an Informal Mindfulness Practice," *Mindfulness* 6 (2015): doi. org/10.1007/s12671-014-0360-9.

3 Adam Brady, "Nature Therapy: How Nature Can Help Heal and Expand Your Awareness," Chopra, April 17, 2018, chopra.com/articles/ nature-therapy-how-nature-can-help-heal-and-expand-your-awareness.

4 Russ Harris, ACT *with Love: Stop Struggling, Reconcile Differences, and Strengthen Your Relationship with Acceptance and Commitment Therapy* (Oakland, CA: New Harbinger, 2009).

5 Dan Diamond, "Just 8% of People Achieve Their New Year's Resolutions. Here's How They Do It," *Forbes*, January 1, 2013, forbes.com/sites/ dandiamond/2013/01/01/just-8-of-people-achieve-their-new-years-resolutions-heres-how-they-did-it/#13070945596b.

6 Allistair McCaw, "New Year's Day Edition: Nothing Changes Unless You Do!" *Champion Minded* (podcast), 17:05, December 31, 2019, championminded. libsyn.com/new-years-day-edition-nothing-changes-unless-you-do.

7 Phillippa Lally, Cornelia H. M. van Jaarsveld, Henry W. W. Potts, and Jane Wardle, "How Habits Are Formed: Modelling Habit Formation in the Real World," *European Journal of Social Psychology* 40, no. 6 (2010): doi. org/10.1002/ejsp.674.

Chapter 10: Humour

1 Goodreads, s.v. "Mark Twain Quotes," goodreads.com/quotes/ 251745-humor-is-the-great-thing-the-saving-thing-the-minute.

2 Alexandra Michel, "The Science of Humour Is No Laughing Matter," *Observer* magazine, Association for Psychological Science, March 31, 2017, psychologicalscience.org/observer/the-science-of-humor-is-no-laughing-matter.

3   Robin Dunbar et al., "Social Laughter Is Correlated with an Elevated Pain Threshold," *Proceedings of the Royal Society B* 279, no. 1731 (2011): doi. org/10.1098/rspb.2011.1373; Pallab Ghosh, "Study Reveals Laughter Really Is the Best Medicine," BBC News, September 14, 2011, bbc.com/ news/science-environment-14889165.

4   Margarita Tartakovsky, "The Importance of Play for Adults," *Psych Central*, last updated July 8, 2018, psychcentral.com/blog/the-importance-of-play-for-adults/.

5   Pamela Paresky, *A Year of Kindness: Discover How Journaling about Kindness Leads to a Happier, More Meaningful Life* (self-published, 2011), ayearof kindness.com.

6   Viktor Frankl, *Man's Search for Meaning*, new edition (London, UK: Rider Books, 2011).

7   Ibid.

8   Goodreads, s.v. "Fred Rogers Quotes," goodreads.com/quotes/198594-when-i-was-a-boy-and-i-would-see-scary.

Chapter 11: The Resiliency Trajectory Model

1   Jerry L. Patterson and Paul Kelleher, *Resilient School Leaders: Strategies for Turning Adversity into Achievement* (Alexandria, VA: Association for Supervision and Curriculum Development, 2005), ascd.org/Publications/ Books/Overview/Resilient-School-Leaders.aspx.

2   Christopher Vogel, "A Practical Guide to *The Hero with a Thousand Faces*," Raindance, April 1, 2013, raindance.org/a-practical-guide-to-the-hero-with-a-thousand-faces/.

Chapter 12: The Four Phases

1   Lawrence Robinson, Melinda Smith, and Jeanne Segal, "Emotional and Psychological Trauma," HelpGuide, helpguide.org/articles/ptsd-trauma/ coping-with-emotional-and-psychological-trauma.htm.

2   Ken Druck, "11 Things to Remember When Coping with Tragedy," MindBodyGreen, September 20, 2017, mindbodygreen.com/articles/ 11-things-to-remember-when-youre-coping-with-tragedy.

3   Trish Loehr, "PhD Student Uses Indigenous Ways of Knowing, Being and Doing to Find Healing from Child Sexual Abuse," *UCalgary News*, University of Calgary, May 27, 2019, ucalgary.ca/news/phd-student-uses-indigenous-ways-knowing-being-and-doing-find-healing-child-sexual-abuse.

4   Margarita Tartakovsky, "8 Creative Activities to Discover Your Values," *Psych Central*, June 10, 2019, psychcentral.com/blog/8-creative-activities-to-discover-your-values/; for more activities by Benke, see her book *Rip All the Pages! 52 Tear-Out Adventures for Creative Writers* (Boulder, CO: Roost Books, 2019).

5   Carley Hauck, "4 Questions to Foster Your Authentic Self," Leading from Wholeness, October 17, 2016, carleyhauck.com/2016/10/17/4-questions-foster-authentic-self/.

6   Goodreads, s.v. "Bill Watterson Quotes," goodreads.com/quotes/808267-creating-a-life-that-reflects-your-values-and-satisfies-your.

7   You can find a list of common core values on James Clear's website: jamesclear.com/core-values.

8   Sir Ken Robinson has a terrific TED Talk called "Do Schools Kills Creativity?" that highlights this idea: ted.com/talks/sir_ken_robinson_do_schools_kill_creativity/transcript?language=en.

Chapter 13: Worth

1   Gabor Maté, *The Return to Ourselves: Trauma, Healing, and the Myth of Normal* (Boulder, CO: Sounds True, 2018), 6 compact discs.

2   Kimberly Miller, "Reclaiming Your Inherent Self-Worth," *Psych Central*, October 8, 2018, https://psychcentral.com/lib/reclaiming-your-inherent-self-worth/.

Conclusion: Lighthouses

1   Goodreads, s.v. "Viktor E. Frankl Quotes," goodreads.com/author/quotes/2782.Viktor_E_Frankl.

2   Goodreads, s.v. "Viktor E. Frankl Quotes," goodreads.com/quotes/460507-to-draw-an-analogy-a-man-s-suffering-is-similar-to.

3   Viktor Frankl, *Man's Search for Meaning,* new edition (London, UK: Rider Books, 2011).

4   Goodreads, s.v. "Buckminster Fuller Quotes," goodreads.com/quotes/ 10107462-what-is-my-job-on-the-planet-what-is-it.

INDEX

Note: Page numbers in italics refer to figures

A Game of Thrones (Martin), 74-75

A-game, 57-58

acceptance, 143-57, 169, 201-2; action questions and, 145; as choice, 152, 154; emotions as teachers, 154-57; inability to reach, 148-49; journaling and, 151-52; living examined life and, 150-52; negative self-talk and, 149; radical, 155-56; readiness for, 146, 148; resistance vs. persistence, 169; takes time, 151; "why" questions and, 144, 151

acceptance and commitment therapy (ACT), 166; acceptance, 169; cognitive defusion and, 168; commitment, 171-72; mindfulness and, 166-68; self as context, 169; values-driven living, 170-71

accident: author's account of, 20-22; author's survival as miracle, 14-15; Joseph saved author, 26

Achor, Shawn, 60

ACT Made Simple (Harris), 166

actionable outcome: values list and, 170

adapt phase, adverse event, 224-30

adverse event: adapt phase, 224-30; Alissa the teacher, 222-24; Andrew comes back, 237-38, 240-41; author's Mom's passing, 226-29; decline phase, 219-24; four phases of, 219-41; prompts for responding to, 220; psychological trauma, signs of, 219-20; reclaim phase, 231-35; rise phase, 235-37

age of worry, 38-39

"aha" moments, 146

Ainsworth, Mary, 108

Albrecht, Karl, 70

Alias Grace (Atwood), 111

Alissa the teacher, 222-24

Always Looking Up (Fox), 143

Andrew comes back, 237-38, 240-41

Angelou, Maya, 26

anxiety, box breathing for, 81, 82

Aristotle, 144

Asher, Terrilee, 90

association stigma, 92

Atomic Habits (Clear), 140, 236

attachment theory, 108

attitude, mindset and, 126–27

Aurelius, Marcus, 29

authenticity, 96–97; disarming shame with, 98–99

Axe body products, 247, 248

barriers to resiliency, 44–45; fear, 67–85; stigma, 87–101; stress, 49–66

behaviour. *See* helping behaviour

belonging, 105–23; attachment theory, 108; community connection, 117–20; connection, finding, 113–20; faith and, 120–23; joining vs. building, 118–19; longevity and, 107; need for, and social pain, 110–13; prisoner's story of, 111; roles and, 108–9; safety network, 115, 117; self-connection, 113–17; the stories we carry, 108–10

Benke, Karen, 233

best practices vs. wise practices, 44

big ideas: Part I, 40–41, 43–45; Part II, 99, 101; Part III, 201–3; Part IV, 253–55

Blue Zones research initiative, 107, 120

The Body Keeps the Score (van der Kolk), 155

boiling frog fable, 40–41

books, value of, 39

Bowlby, John, 108

box breathing, 81, 82

boxers, professional, supports for, 117

Brady, Adam, 167–68

Brady, Tom, 136, 148, 150

branding humans, 88, 90

Brazil, Inti, 69

breastfeeding mom, 108

Brown, Brené, 94, 96–97; belonging, 105; values list, 236

Buettner, Dan, 107

bullying, author's experience of, 18

Bulten, Eric, 69

busyness, as coping strategy, 83

butterfly breathing, 81–82

call to adventure, resiliency and, 214, 216

Cameron, Julia, 152

Campbell, Joseph, 214

Campbell, Nicole, 238

Can't Hurt Me (Goggins), 83–84

Canadian Mental Health Association (CMHA): definition of stress, 56

cancel culture, 34; self-harm and, 36

cardinal virtues, 76

caring companion champion, 115

Carlie, Michael, 111

Carnegie, Dale, 77

Carpenter, Maggie (*Runaway Bride*), 113–14
Champion Minded (McCaw), 172
children: frightened by stress, 51, 53–54; hope, and, 174–79; talking to and inner dialogue, 165
Chittister, Sister Joan, 54–55
Clear, James, 140, 236
CMHA (Canadian Mental Health Association): definition of stress, 56
cognitive behavioural therapy (CBT), 145
cognitive defusion, 168
Coloroso, Barbara, 134
commitment, 171–72
community connections: making, 117–20; starting small, examples, 119–20
conditional self-worth, 248
connection: community, 117–20; finding, 113–20; need for, 112; with self, 113–17
controllables, 202
core values, 235–37
Corrigan, Patrick W., 91, 93
courtesy stigma, 92
COVID-19, 53
criticism: as judgement, 33–34; as self-criticism, 34
Crum, Alia, 60

Dare to Lead (Brown), 236
Dass, Ram, 2
Davidson, Marlina, 67
De Rosa, Wendy, 156
decline phase, 254; adverse event, 219–24
defusion, 145

depression as attacker of hope, 159
derailment in high school, 18
dialectical behaviour therapy (DBT), 155–57
disease to please, 232–33
distress, 64–65; zone of, 58
Dodson, John Dillingham, 57
Dove Campaign for Real Beauty, 247–48
Doyle, Glennon, 56
dragons, slaying, as resiliency, 216–17
Druck, Ken, 220
Dunbar, Robin, 184
Dweck, Carol, 38, 126
Dwyer, Karen, 67

education, as learning in motion, 26
Eisenberger, Naomi, 112, 117
emotion and mindset, 127–28
emotional health problems, medication and, 160
emotions as teachers, 154–57
empathic attunement, 107
eustress (good stress), 58
everyday fear, 83–85
examined life, living, 150–52

failing-forward, 135
faith, 120–23; prayer and belonging, 122
false beliefs, 251; create new experience/evidence, 252–53; identifying and redefining, 251, 252

fear, 67–85; in action, 81–83; as barrier, 72–74; box breathing, 81, 82; childhood experiences, 70–71; courage and, 66; ego protection and, 84–85; everyday, 83–85; excitement and, 69; parental, passing on to children, 71–72; as stress, 68–71; visualization, 81–82

fear-setting, 75–83; exercise, 76–77, 78–79; knowing what you can control, 76; living by virtue, 76; living in agreement with nature, 76; Stoicism and, 75–76

feararchy, 70

Ferriss, Tim, 75

The Five-Minute Journal, 152

Flynn, Alison, 238

forgiveness, importance of, 265

four phases. See adverse event

Fox, Michael J., 143

Frankl, Viktor, 39, 193–94, 263–65

Fuller, Buckminster, 266

gaslighting, author's experience of, 18

gender equality, and coaching basketball team, 177–78

The Gifts of Imperfection (Brown), 94

global health pandemic, 53

Goggins, David, 83–84

gratitude, 138, 140–41, 152

grief, laughter and, 186–87

growth mindset, 38

guilt vs. shame, 93

habit-stacking, 138, 140–41

habits, forming new ones, 172

Hanley, Lesley, 226–29

Hanley-Dafoe, Ava Lesley: butterfly breathing, 81–82; cross-country race perspective, 129–32; finding mom's joy, 189

Hanley-Dafoe, Hunter: basketball championships, 174–76; basketball skills, 126; coaching Jaxson, 197–99; and St. Jude, 191

Hanley-Dafoe, Jaxson: basketball team needs coach, 176–79; basketball team selection, 196–99; hungry at school, 249–50; jokes, 185, 186–87

Hanley-Dafoe, Robyne: coaching basketball team, 177–78; experience of bullying, 18; family motto, 97; fear of birds, 71–72; institutionalized, 160; lighthouses and, 257–58, 261–62; mother's passing, 226–29, 235–36; negative feelings and emotional decline, 15–16; negative self-talk, 17–18; Scottish roots, 258–59; service, living life of, 24; shamed on morning walk, 95–96; stories we are told, 231–32; tattoo for loved one, 154; TED Talk, 182; things bringing joy, 190–92

Harris, Russ, 166, 170

Hauck, Carley, 234

head-heart connection, resiliency and, 41, 43-45
heavy heart work, 65
helicopter parenting, 135
helping behaviour, stress reduc-
tion and, 64-65
The Hero with a Thousand Faces
(Campbell), 214
hero's journey, resiliency as, 214
holding space, 99
hope, 159-79, 202; child's
point of view, 174-79; as
choice, 163-64; finding, 161,
163-64; lessons of, 172, 174;
soldiers' unfinished projects
and, 163; tools for choosing and building, 166-72;
transformational thinking
and, 164-72
Hoppenbrouwers, Sylco, 69
humour, 181-200, 202; author's
constellation of, 183-94; author's intention re chapter,
199; concerns about using,
181, 182; don't take life
too seriously, 196; finding
anywhere, 196-99; laughter
and, 184-87; wonder and
awe, 192-94

identity, roles and, 109-9
immune systems: finding,
185-86; laughter and, 185
imposter syndrome, 112
Indigenous ways of knowing,
44
inherent wholeness, 248
inner dialogue/speech, 164-65

Jagged Little Pill (Morissette), 19
JmStorm (poet), 41
Jordan, Michael, 136
journaling, 151, 166; morning
pages practice (Cameron),
152
joy: author's list, 190-92; finding, 189-92
judgement: as coping strategy,
33-34; shame and, 94-95
Jung, Carl, 34

Kelleher, Paul, 208
Kingston Penitentiary, 110-11
knowing what you can control,
76

labels, identity and, 109
laughter, 184-87; in animals,
184; finding joy, 189-92;
grief and, 186-87; as natural
painkiller, 184-85; play and,
187-89; universality of, 184
Laumann, Silken, 13
lawnmower parenting, 135
learning perspective, 135-36
Lieberman, Matthew, 112, 117
lighthouses, 257-67; author's
list of, 261-62; finding your
"why"/way, 263-65; map-
ping our own, 259, 261; PEI
search for, 257-58
living by virtue, 76
living in agreement with nature,
76
logotherapy, 194, 263-65
longevity: belonging and, 107;
faith and, 120-23
love, importance of, 265

"Man in the Arena" speech
(Roosevelt), 198
Man's Search for Meaning
(Frankl), 193–94, 265–66
margarine, 51
Marks, Grace, 111
Martin, George R. R., 74–75
Maté, Gabor, 248
McCaw, Allistair, 172
McGonigal, Kelly, 59, 63
medication, role of, 160
Mee, Benjamin, 75
mental health, 18; stigma and,
22, 93
mental health clinics, 30
military, belonging and, 107.
See also soldiers
Miller, Kimberly, 249
mindfulness: dishwashing
study, 167; stress perception
and, 59; as turning inward,
166–68; walking in nature,
167–68; where to practice,
167
mindset, emotion and, 125–28
Mindset (Dweck), 125–26
Mizpah, 108
mother and baby bond, 107–8
Mr. Rogers, 196

negative feelings, author's emotional decline and, 15–16
negative self-talk, 148, 149;
author's, 17–18
negative thoughts, script to
counter, 23–24
Neuberg, Steven, 90
nighttime, negative self-talk
and, 17–18

Nin, Anaïs, 84
non-intact family, 92

O'Hagan, Fergal, 169
O'Shaughnessy, John R., 91
Obama, Barack, 34–35
otherness/outsider, author's
feelings re, 16–17

pain, philosophers describe, 29
parental resiliency, 188–89
parents, new, empathic attunement, 107
Paresky, Pamela, 193
Patterson, Jerry, 208
Pennebaker, James, 151–52
personal sliming, 36
perspective, 125–41, 201; in
action, 133–34; "aha" mo-
ments, 146; habit-stacking,
138, 140–41; language and,
133–34; learning, 135–36;
little but mighty shift in,
129–32; mental nimbleness
and, 133; mighty shift in,
128–29; mindfulness and,
141; mindset and, 125–28;
practical, 134–35; sharp-
ening, 136–38; to-be lists,
137–38
play: laughter and, 187–89; as
state of mind, 188
positive psychology movement,
30–31, 32
positive stress experience, 58
post-traumatic stress disorder
(PTSD), 129
Poulin, Michael, stress and
helping behaviour, 64–65

prayer, 122
psychological research, funding
    for, 30
psychological trauma, symp-
    toms of, 219–20
The Psychology of Hope (Snyder),
    164

Qubein, Nido, 74

R. H. Bruskin Associates, 67
radical acceptance, 155–56
Rao, Deepa, 93
reclaim phase, adverse event,
    231–35; personal guideposts,
    234–35; questions to ask
    yourself, 233–34
reframing, 145
relational aggression, 94–95
resiliency, 201; barriers to (*see*
    barriers to resiliency);
    belonging and, 105–24;
    big ideas of Part I, 40–41,
    43–45; experiences and
    inner strength, 122–23;
    fostering with wonder
    and awe, 194; head-heart
    connection and, 41, 43–45;
    historical definition of, 29;
    humour and, 181–200, 202;
    inner strength and,122–23;
    parental, 188–89; personal
    perspective-taking and,
    125–41; redefined, 32–33;
    social equity and, 202–3;
    wise practices and, 44
resiliency redefined, 29–40;
    defining resiliency, 32–33;
    social comparison, blast
    radius of, 33–40

resiliency research, 29–30, 32
Resiliency Trajectory Model,
    201–17, *208*, 253–54; adapt
    phase, 211–12; decline phase,
    209, 211; reclaim phase, 212;
    rise phase, 212–13
Resiliency Trajectory Model
    Sample, *213*
Resilient School Leaders (Patter-
    son and Kelleher), 208
rise phase, adverse event,
    235–41; Andrew comes back,
    237–41; core values and,
    235–37
Roberts, Julia, 113–14
Rocky (film franchise), 117
roles, identity and, 108–9
Roosevelt, Theodore, 198
Rose, Tania, 69
Runaway Bride, 113–14

safety network, 115, 117
Salovey, Peter, 60
Scotland, author's forebears
    emigrated from, 258–59
self as context, 169
self-acceptance, 156–57
self-compassion, 23
self-connection, 113, 117
self-efficacy, 7, 201, 208–14
self-esteem: contingent vs.
    genuine, 248; rewriting
    your stories and, 251–52; as
    self-worth, 247–53; social
    comparison and, 35–36; stig-
    ma and, 93
self-forgiveness, 156–57
self-harm, author's dragon, 216
self-help books not helpful, 37

self-improvement, seeking,
36–37
self-narrative, negative feelings
and, 16
self-reflection, questions for,
114–15
self-regulation, inner speech
and, 165
self-worth: conditional, 248;
self-esteem and, 247–53
Seligman, Martin, 30
Seneca, 29, 83
sentence, the, 13–27; author's,
22
service, life of, 24
shame: disarming with authenticity, 98–99; explained, 94;
stigma and, 93–98
shaming, 94–95; as relational
aggression, 94
single parent, custody battle,
216
single-parent family, stigma
and, 92
sitting in discomfort, 99, 101
Smith, Dylan, 90
sniper breathing, 82–83
snowplow parenting, 135–36
Snyder, Charles R., 164
social comparison, 35; blast
radius of, 33–40; crisis of
disconnection and, 36;
finding answers for, 36–39;
invitation to change, 39–40;
judgement and criticism,
33–35; low self-esteem and,
35–36; upward and down-
ward, 35
social determinants of health,
16

social equity, resiliency and,
202–3
social media: comparisons and,
34; as distraction, 112
social pain: need to belong and,
110–13; rejection and, 117
Socrates, 144–45
soldiers: conversations with,
161, 163; empathic attunement, 107; feelings about
shortness, 148–50; hope
and reconnection, 161,
163–64; post-traumatic
growth example, 128–29;
sniper breathing, 82–83
Springsteen, Bruce, 38
St-Denis, Natalie, 231
Stallone, Sylvester, 191
stigma, 87–101; association
(courtesy), 92; author's experience of, 14–15; as barrier
to resiliency, 22–23; branding humans, 88, 90; defined,
88; effects of, 92–99; elitism
and, 90; emotions and, 156;
forms of, 91–92; as intended
mark, 90; letting go of, 98;
mental health and, 93; self,
92; social, 91; structured, 91
Stoicism, 75–76
stories: author told herself, 15;
belonging and, 108–10;
rewriting, 251–53
Strayed, Cheryl, 72
stress, 49–65; arousal and, 57;
as barrier to resiliency,
49–66; body's response to,
58; children and, 51, 53–54;
climate change and, 53–54;
CMHA definition of, 55;

COVID-19 and, 53; definition of, 51–56; eustress, 58; in families, 53; fear as, 68–71; helping behaviour and, 64–65; perception of, and health, 59–60; performance and, 56–58; positive experience of, 58; productive beliefs about, 63; rejecting harmful effects of, 63–64; revisiting our understanding of, 59–65; students', 49–50; teacher's, 49–50; traditional medical model definition of, 55–56
Stress Mindset Measure (SMM), 60–62, 64; examples, 62–63; questions re, 61
students, 49–50
suffering, logotherapy and, 263–65

tattoos, 88, 90
teachers, 49–50; unkind words of, 15
TED Talk, author's, 182
therapy, acceptance and, 146
thoughts, repetitive, 263
Threads of Life, 65
The Time Is Now (Chittister), 54–55
to-be lists, 137–38
transformational thinking: defined, 165; hope and, 164–72. See also acceptance and commitment therapy
Twain, Mark, 183

Unsinkable, 13
Untamed (Doyle), 56
The Upside of Stress (McGonigal), 59, 63

value word sets, 236–37
values: core, 235–37; list, 170; word sets, 236–37
values-driven living, 170–71
van der Kolk, Bessel, 155
visualization, butterflies, 81–82
Vygotsky, Lev, 165

warning messages, tempering, 172, 174
wholeness, inherent, 248
"why" questions, 144, 151
winning your mornings, 95–96
wise practices vs. best practices, 44
Witt, Whitney P., stress study, 59–60
wonder and awe, 192–94
World Health Organization (WHO): social determinants of health, definition of, 16
worth, 243–55, 243–55; know yours, 245–47; self-esteem as self-worth, 247–53

Year of Kindness (Paresky), 193
Yerkes-Dodson Human Performance and Stress Curve, 56–57, 57
Yerkes, Robert, 57
yoga mountain pose, 168

zone of distress, 58

Rebekah Littlejohn

ABOUT THE AUTHOR

DR. ROBYNE HANLEY-DAFOE is a multi-award-winning psychology and education instructor who specializes in resiliency, navigating stress and change, leadership, and personal wellness in the workplace. Robyne's writing and speaking interests focus on resiliency and wellness, in her own backyard and around the world. She has worked within post-secondary education in a variety of roles, bringing wise practices for professional development, research, learning, and authentic change.

Robyne is committed to finding sustainable solutions for creating positive relationships for individuals, teachers, families, and organizations. Robyne would be the first person to tell you she is still navigating her way through all the research and literature, talking with people and exploring, with the intention of developing a deeper understanding of resiliency. Her refreshing approach looks at resiliency from multiple vantage points with the aim of being fully accessible to everyone.

Robyne lives in Central Ontario with her husband and three amazing children, who remind her each day that she still has a lot to learn about mostly everything! On most days Robyne runs on her love of historical fiction, coffee, and puppies —oh, and a clean kitchen in the morning.

WORK WITH DR. ROBYNE HANLEY-DAFOE

Described as transformational, engaging, and thought-provoking, Robyne's keynotes provide practical strategies grounded in global research and case studies that help foster resiliency within ourselves. Regardless of your background or prior knowledge, you will find Robyne's work relatable, approachable, and rooted in honest personal reflection and humour. She guides you along your journey with research-informed wise practices that you can adapt and adopt in your own life.

Robyne is available for consultation, training, and professional development opportunities ranging from one-on-one to company-wide initiatives.

robynehd.ca
@dr_robynehd
@rhanleydafoe